Zen & the Path *of* *Mindful* Parenting

Meditations on Raising Children

Clea Danaan

Leaping Hare Press

This edition published in the UK and North America in 2016 by

Leaping Hare Press

Ovest House, 58 West Street
Brighton BN1 2RA, UK
www.quartoknows.com

First published in the UK in 2015

British Library Cataloguing-in-Publication Data
A catalogue record for this book is available from
the British Library

ISBN: 978-1-78240-154-4

This book was conceived, designed and produced by

Leaping Hare Press

Creative Director PETER BRIDGEWATER
Publisher SUSAN KELLY
Editorial Director TOM KITCH
Art Director WAYNE BLADES
Commissioning Editor MONICA PERDONI
Project Editor JOANNA BENTLEY
Designer GINNY ZEAL
Illustrator SARAH YOUNG

Printed in China

1 3 5 7 9 10 8 6 4 2

CONTENTS

INTRODUCTION

We all strive so hard to be the perfect parents
— we do whatever it takes to assure our children's
happiness and safety, and that they will grow up to
be their best selves. Unfortunately, though, our striving
is making us crazy. Being a helicopter or tiger mum
(or dad) drains us and harms our health. Such an
approach may very well harm our kids, too. So how can
we raise happy, healthy children while staying happy
and healthy ourselves? How can we take the crazy-
making out of parenting — and life in general
— and reawaken a heart-centred family life?

THE JOURNEY OF PARENTING

◆

The key to living a joyful parenting life isn't yet another manual — and this book is not intended as such. The last thing you need is another expert telling you the 'right' way to do it. All we really need is a circle of friends, who have our backs and our hearts.

SOME OF MY FAVOURITE MOMENTS as a parent are simply sitting with other parents over tea or coffee, and talking. As our children play out in the garden or at the other end of the room, we tell stories and offer support. We cry and laugh and pick apart challenges until we feel we can go on again. Or at least we feel not so alone on our journey as parents. Someone understands, and has been there, too.

My intention for *Zen and the Path of Mindful Parenting* is for this book to be something like those circles of parents over tea. I offer my own stories, plus insights I have gained as I have grown as a parent. For not only are we raising our children, we are raising ourselves into whole new beings. Parenting is a journey, a path to awakening. As a parent on our journey, we will grow ourselves by accepting that this is a 'quest to realize our truest, deepest nature as a human being'.[1]

One of the greatest tools we can carry with us on our quest is the tool of mindfulness. While mindfulness and meditation are part of many religions, as well as secular awareness practices, Zen Buddhists have perfected the art over thousands of years. So to learn from the tool of mindfulness in the path of parenting, we will draw much wisdom from Zen Buddhism.

Zen & Mindfulness

'Zen' simply means meditation. It usually refers — table-top sandpits aside — to a regular practice of zazen, or sitting meditation, done alone or with a group. In traditional zazen, you sit on a special cushion, cross-legged and straight-spined, and let your gaze rest gently in front of you while you follow your breath. The point is not to be calm or even to reach enlightenment (meaning you experience directly the nature of the Universe), but simply to be present in this ever-unfolding moment right now. The practice takes you out of your thoughts, with which we in Western culture (and no doubt other human cultures as well) are so very identified. We believe our thoughts — worries, projections, machinations and plans — to be reality. But in fact they are merely thoughts, tools that we have allowed to take over how we relate to the

---

[Parenting] calls us to recreate our world
every day, to meet it freshly in every moment. Such a
calling is actually nothing less than a rigorous spiritual
discipline — a quest to realize our truest, deepest
nature as a human being.

MYLA AND JON KABAT-ZINN [2]

Everything is amazing right now and nobody's happy.

LOUIS C.K.[3]

world and ourselves. In doing so we have lost our true selves, the higher self or inner wisdom or witness. We have lost touch with the amazingly beautiful ever-unfolding moment.

Becoming aware of our thoughts and of our identification with them is called mindfulness. We become mindful of the moment, of our thoughts, of our breath. We pay attention. When you sit zazen, you have a fairly simplified space in which to pay attention. You have your body and your thoughts. Fairly simple, but not easy to maintain. Mindfulness can also be practised off the cushion, through everyday life. Washing the dishes, you notice. Mowing the lawn, you notice. Feeding the dog, you notice.

And when you bring mindfulness to parenting, you notice.

Applying mindfulness to parenting will change everything else in your life, deeply and for the better.

A Hero's Journey

I discovered early in my parenting journey that parenting is a Hero's Journey, a shamanic death into the heart of our own selves. Like old Zen teachings that draw on stories and myths well known to the listeners, I will use the story of the Hero's Journey to walk us through the path of mindful parenting.

Each section of this book follows the Hero's Journey: The Call, Meeting Yourself, Allies and Obstacles, Finding the Stillness, and Becoming Whole. First we are called to the path of parenting as a mindfulness practice that calls us into a deeper journey, a seeking of greater awareness and personal growth. Along the journey we face the truth about ourselves, which is not always a comfortable process. We meet allies who help us and stumble on obstacles in the road. In the midst of the turmoil, we discover the sweetness of stillness, of noticing where we are and what we are really doing here right now. Finally we return (more or less) triumphant, more whole than we were when we began. We face this journey each day, in cycles of darkness, seeking, and awakening. We face this journey as parents in a changing world.

Along the path we will face our ultimate darkness. Also, however, we will find much light and joy. In each section I have included one or two practices to try on your own and with your children, which I call Playtime. These are ways to joyfully and mindfully awaken with your children into different ways of becoming more present and aware. This path is one that you must walk yourself, but ultimately it is about relationship, not just with yourself, but with those in your life. As a parent, you will of course see this most clearly in relationship with your children.

So lace up your hiking boots, pack extra snacks in the bag, and take a deep breath. Here we go!

CHAPTER ONE

THE CALL

Every journey, like the Hero's Journey,
begins with a call to action, a call to the path. Our
discomfort in life and in parenting calls us to begin to
know ourselves more deeply. Like a child's call beckons
us to play, to pick up the crying baby, or simply to be
in the moment as it arises, we respond to the call
of our deeper selves. We begin by moving towards
mindfulness and greater awareness.

UNPLEASANTNESS

◆

We spend our days avoiding unpleasantness. Certainly, it is human nature to do so. When I am cold, I put on a sweater. When my child is screaming, I want him to stop. Sometimes, though, we cannot avoid unpleasantness. We are then faced with a powerful choice.

THEY'RE BORED. GOD FORBID. Also, we are trying to leave the house, which equals 'transition', which my daughter, at least, is not good at. So my nearly-nine-year-old and my nearly-five-year-old start riffing. Loud, slightly manic, repeated phrases: 'Coconut bananas in my ear!' Hysterical laughter. 'Don't step on my bananas! They're evil bananas!' More hysterical laughter.

My usual response is to yell over them 'Stop! No crazies!' Problem is, this usually fuels the fire. They get even more manic, feeding off my annoyance, feeding off each other, till they are bouncing off the walls. Literally. While shouting random nonsense and laughing like hyenas. And not putting on their shoes, which I have asked them to do three times.

I breathe in slowly. Breathe out. Keep gathering up my things in order to leave the house. Notice my breath, notice the noise they are making without jumping to clenching judgements about the noise.

They put on their shoes, we leave the house, and they stop. And I am calm. Score one for Zen Mummy.

Make It Stop!

We humans tend so often to resist unpleasantness, to want to make it stop. Unpleasantness can look like many things, and one person's unpleasant may not faze someone else. Hyper kids, the buzzing of the dryer, a barking dog, the smoke alarm, the glare of an angry passerby, burned dinner – does your blood pressure rise when you just read these words?

It is the mind that tells us these events are 'bad', whereas soaking in a hot bath before getting a massage is 'good'. Fact is, these events simply *are*. They exist. It is the mind that offers all its assessments, judgements and commentary. And while these comments and judgements are not good or bad, either, we get tripped up when we equate reality and our reactions to it with the machinations of the mind.

The Zen monk and teacher (called a roshi) Shunryu Suzuki said, 'In your very imperfections you will find the basis for your firm way-seeking mind.'[4] In other words, challenges help us grow. We discover this later, when we've survived a difficult passage of life and come out stronger. In the midst of pain and imperfection, it's harder to see. Suzuki Roshi is saying that through the imperfection or unpleasantness itself is where we will find our way. The annoyance of hyper children becomes my personal gritty bit of sand. It is not, however, the sand itself that yields the pearl, it is our *attention* to the grit, over and over again, that will gain us infinite inner wealth, the pearl of awareness.

Buddhism's Four Noble Truths

1. Life is suffering.

2. Suffering has an origin.

3. Suffering can cease.

4. There is a path out of suffering.

There is a misconception that Zen, or meditation in general, is about being unflappable, or calm in every moment. But the point is actually not to be unflappable or calm, the point is simply to become aware of what is happening (which often tends to lead to us being unflappable). This is easy when what is happening is a lovely butterfly settling airily on a pretty flower. Ah, we can breathe, ah, we are so one with all things, one with the butterfly, one with the flower. But this exercises nothing, except an appreciation of beauty. It is in being pushed, noticing that we are being pushed, and then being present that we find our way.

Zen is about accepting that suffering exists. Life is hard. Once you accept this and stop pushing against it by efforting endlessly to make everything easier all the time, a bit of a burden lifts from your shoulders. Which is not to say that you shouldn't pull out a thorn from your foot to end the pain, simply that a lot of our pain comes from our mind's assessments about the thorn.

Noble truth number one, for instance: kids are annoying. Noble truth number two is not, however, that annoying kids are the origin of my suffering. Noble truth number two actually says that the origin of my suffering is my mind's reaction to annoying kids. Suffering can cease (Noble truth number three) when I notice that I create my own reality. When I notice that reality, I follow the path out of my suffering. And more easily out the front door, with two hyper kids who don't like transition, who finally put on their shoes, and I can do it without suffering. At least for the moment.

Zen is about noticing, and it's a practice you have to do yourself. No one can notice things for you. You can read and talk and read some more but until you practise it, either on a meditation cushion or through daily life (or even better, both), you will not discover the truths and freedom on the other side. It doesn't matter what religion you follow; some form of mindfulness is found in all major religions. Mindfulness is about tapping into the human capacity to notice, and through noticing to tease apart unconscious beliefs you have about who you are and what you are doing here.

So right now, in this moment, notice. What is there for you to feel, see, smell, hear, sense? Try noticing or practising mindfulness when something unpleasant happens. Just notice your automatic reaction to it. You might even notice why you have a reaction. Try not to dig too deep at the moment, just notice. Notice your body's reaction to unpleasantness.

AVOIDANCE

One of the ways we deal with unpleasantness is simply to avoid those things that might create unpleasant sensations. What is it that we are avoiding? The pain, the discomfort, or our perceptions about them? What is it that we really fear, and why?

I GIVE MY KIDS A FIVE-MINUTE WARNING: we will be leaving the children's museum in five minutes. I ask my two-year-old pointedly but gently to please put away the fabric carrots in the pretend garden. Would you like to put them in this basket or in the holes in the pretend ground? I stand, smiling, and slip the strap of the nappy bag over one shoulder. Okay, I say in a very friendly voice, time to go!

Despite my careful planning and preparations, she throws herself to the floor and screams.

I imagine that as a parent you might have been here too, with a toddler or a preschooler or a thirteen-year-old, one who tends to react so strongly to something not going her way that she explodes. The blast of emotion coming from your little one when her favourite socks are dirty, or she can't get a certain toy, or it's time to leave her best friend's house, or you are out of frozen waffles – this blast so rocks your world that you will do anything to stop it. You fear that you are raising a spoiled brat. You know you should stay calm. So you draw boundaries, punish, or talk about feelings; you do whatever your approach to parenting (or your friends' approach or the latest book you read) urges you to do in order to make the unpleasantness stop.

The fight, and the anticipation of that fight, is exhausting. You're so tired of being tired. You just don't know what to do!

Be Present to Your Sensations

Much of parenting, from our trying to shape well-behaved children to avoiding scraped knees, is spent avoiding pain and discomfort, for who wants to see her child suffer? The truth is, pain and suffering are a part of life. We do ourselves and our children a disservice by putting so much effort into avoiding that suffering. *The exhausting bit is not the explosion, it's the fear of and avoidance of and reaction to the explosion.* The beautiful thing is that these aspects – the fear, avoidance, and our inner reaction – these are all in our minds. And we can shift these stories and reactions not by doing anything with our minds, but by becoming more present. What we need to do is notice what is and stop avoiding our own discomfort.

I'm not here to belittle anything you or I have experienced as a parent. Parenting can be exhausting. Some of it is truly horrendous – losing a child or fearing for their life or dealing with a disability can be terrifying and overwhelming. But I invite you to just play with the idea of becoming aware of what is actually happening. I invite you to become present to your sensations. Be open to what happens next.

Whose Distress Is It?

I overheard a mother in a ladies' room one day dealing with a dirty nappy. The boy was about two, and had apparently avoided telling his mother about his soiled pants, and was then crying inconsolably as she changed him. I empathized with her; when my daughter was a toddler she was terrified of public changing tables and screamed when I had to use them. In this case, though, I have to say I felt for the boy. The mother repeatedly told her distraught son, 'Stop acting like that – you are fine! You're just fine! Stop it!' as she wrestled him onto the changing table. I felt for her, too – she was clearly embarrassed, tired, annoyed.

Sometimes children need assurance that they are fine. You aren't bleeding, it's just a scratch, we tell them, and up they go, off to their friends, the scratch forgotten. This boy, however, was clearly not soothed by his mother's assurance, which quickly turned to scolding. For the words were not about his distress – they were about hers.

Again, we've all been there – myself oh so many times. And we try to remember what we're supposed to do, reflecting their feelings and drawing boundaries and whatever else, but the fact is, we want the embarrassing screaming to stop. We want to leave the ladies' room, supermarket or children's museum with a happy mummy and a happy child, everyone well-behaved. No embarrassing moments, no ear-splitting screaming, no tantrum.

So the crux … is this: all we must do is
constantly to create a little shift from the spinning
world we've got in our heads to right-here-now.

CHARLOTTE JOKO BECK [5]

The Secret of Success

The secret to avoiding embarrassment and pain is not to avoid it and push it away, however, but to become so very aware of your experience that your awareness transforms that inner experience completely. Suddenly, there is no embarrassment. The screaming is a noise, one that you gently suspect will pass in a few minutes. The screaming/tantrum/anger/pain is no longer an impediment to your having the perfect life and being the ideal parent, it just exists. It is no longer in control of the moment, for the moment unfolds of its own accord.

My daughter got mad the other day at her rainbow loom, a little device that helps her turn tiny coloured rubber bands into trendy bracelets. She did something wrong and the whole thing unravelled. She threw it on the floor with an angry yell, stomped off to her room, and slammed the door. For the next ten minutes she wailed and cried and yelled, throwing stuffed animals at the wall and stomping on the floor. Part of me wanted to go tell her to knock it off already. Really? I wanted to say. All of this drama because your rubber bands aren't cooperating? But I didn't. I let her wail and scream, keeping a

bit of attention to the noise to ensure she didn't hurt herself. And when she came out of her room, she was spent and calm and in a fairly good mood. I gave her a hug and we went on with our day. By not avoiding her anger or making her stifle it, I sent her the message that she is okay no matter what. That I am here and I love her. And we both survived just fine.

Once you are present to the moment, the stories in your mind about your screaming child and your failures or other's impressions of those failures melt away. They simply do not exist, for they are ungraspable unrealities living only in your mind. When you enter right-here-now, everything lets go.

The irony is, if you *try* to relax, try to get your child to relax, try to do anything but stay present, you can't relax. If you try to avoid an unpleasant situation, it's there in your face. The trick is sort of untrying – falling into the present moment, the right-here-now, accepting, witnessing – the doorway to which is your five senses. What do you hear? What does your clothing feel like on your skin? What is your breath doing? Do you have any taste in your mouth? If you focus on these sensations, you become present.

Once you are present to the moment,
the stories in your mind about your screaming
child and your failures or other's impressions
of those failures melt away.

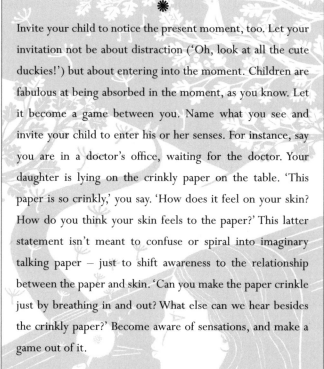

PLAYTIME EXERCISE

SENSATIONS

✳

Invite your child to notice the present moment, too. Let your invitation not be about distraction ('Oh, look at all the cute duckies!') but about entering into the moment. Children are fabulous at being absorbed in the moment, as you know. Let it become a game between you. Name what you see and invite your child to enter his or her senses. For instance, say you are in a doctor's office, waiting for the doctor. Your daughter is lying on the crinkly paper on the table. 'This paper is so crinkly,' you say. 'How does it feel on your skin? How do you think your skin feels to the paper?' This latter statement isn't meant to confuse or spiral into imaginary talking paper – just to shift awareness to the relationship between the paper and skin. 'Can you make the paper crinkle just by breathing in and out? What else can we hear besides the crinkly paper?' Become aware of sensations, and make a game out of it.

VULNERABILITY

Vulnerability means opening ourselves to input from the world. It can be frightening, opening up to sensations and emotions that might be uncomfortable. Opening our hearts and sensitivities, however, is one way we can connect with others. I've never felt more vulnerable, or more connected, than as a parent.

MY FOUR-YEAR-OLD HAS BEEN VOMITING for more than two days now. I'm waiting for the doctor's office to open so I can call for an appointment. No one else has been sick in our family. Taken all together, his symptoms, his age, and the fact that only he has fallen ill, it's easy to start imagining the worst. My husband works for a children's hospital. My high school boyfriend died of leukemia, discovered after his flu-like symptoms wouldn't go away. I know what can happen.

I picture myself sitting in a hospital room, my small, sweet boy attached to tubes and monitors, fighting for his precious little life. The image brings me to tears.

Probably he just has a horrible case of gastroenteritis, I assure myself. But my mind wants to do something with this horrible sense of helplessness. I do whatever I know to — giving him clear fluids, sipped. Dry toast, nibbled. Combing the internet with search phrases like 'When to take a four-year-old into the doctor' and 'current gastroenteritis symptoms'. Prayer. Reiki.

Mostly, the search results say, you just have to wait it out. Which is something the mind just isn't very good at.

Noticing Your Self

Parenting makes us vulnerable in ways we've never felt before. To love someone as profoundly as we do our children opens us to new avenues of weakness. We confront our weakness when a child is sick. In other, less dramatic and obvious ways, too, parenthood brings us up against our own vulnerability, uncovering our human weaknesses. Oh, parenting, how do you push me into my darkest spaces?

In this way, parenting is a lot like sitting meditation.

When you first begin noticing yourself, either on the meditation cushion or in everyday life, you see all those bits of yourself that you were sure didn't exist. Sure, everyone has a bad day now and then. But you don't consider yourself an angry, bitter, judgemental person. Obviously those traits belong to *other* people, not you.

The problem is that when we don't care at
all what people think and we're immune to hurt,
we're also ineffective at connecting. … Staying
vulnerable is a risk we have to take if we
want to experience connection.

BRENÉ BROWN [6]

Then you sit, or notice yourself in a moment, and you see. Oh. My thoughts, with which I often identify, are in fact rather ugly. I think nasty things about my neighbours, friends, husband and children. I beat myself up about everything. I circle around in spinning, barely conscious thoughts about how not enough I am – and I project those thoughts on to others. Most especially the most important people in the world, my children.

Parenting makes us responsible for these people who are at once wholly separate people and yet simultaneously extensions and mirrors of ourselves. We cannot control them or their behaviour. We cannot control whether or not they get sick, if they grow up to be delinquents, or how happy they are. Our children are their own selves. As much as we want to be all-powerful, ultimately we are not in control. That can be humbling and terrifying.

Breathe Through the Fear

Whether we face the fear of losing a child, the pain of not being enough, or the shame of our own shortcomings, our mind fights the feeling of vulnerability. Then we have two choices: to contract, ignore, turn away from the pain of being open and vulnerable – or to go into the pain through gentle mindfulness. We can choose not to shut the door on our own vulnerability. We walk into being vulnerable, knowing that we might be hurt, and breathing through the fear.

When you make this profound choice, to allow yourself to inhabit your state of vulnerability, several things happen. You come face to face with your own selfhood. This is not a comfortable place to sit. We sit in the dizzying realization that we *are*. Really sitting in the existential *isness* of life causes a sort of vertigo. Then, sitting vulnerable and present in your existence, something crazy happens. You slip, for just a moment or two, into the non-material *whatness* that is beyond this material life. Beyond, within, and through this life. It is the space of prayer, the Tao. In the moment of experiencing your vulnerability, you taste for just one tiny slice of the 'now' the dizzying and nonsensical nature of being. In that space, you can truly be with someone, be that person your child, friend, or spouse. Ultimately, this is what we all really seek in relationships, for another person to truly be with us, vulnerable, real, and present.

All's Well That Ends Well

The doctor's office finally opened, and the receptionist agreed I should probably bring my son in to be checked out. He naturally began feeling better in the time between the phone call

---

> Vulnerability means I won't shut
>
> the door even though I am being hurt.
>
> CHARLOTTE JOKO BECK[7]

PLAYTIME EXERCISE
WORRY STICK

We all sometimes need a tangible place to put our worries. Then we can meditate on them without ruminating and then let go what we cannot control. Gather a stick about as thick as your thumb and five or six inches long (around 15 cm), maybe on a nature walk or just in the garden. Collect some wool in a colour that appeals to you. Now sit with your stick, thinking about or talking about something that is bothering you. As you talk (to yourself or a trusted friend) or think, wrap the wool slowly and carefully around the stick until it covers the middle two-thirds of the stick. Tie the wool in a knot and cut it. When you tie off the wool, let your thoughts go.

Set your worry stick on your altar or a windowsill for a few days. When you are ready, bury or burn the wool-covered stick, releasing your concerns and knowing that your Higher Power is doing all it can to make things right.

and the appointment. The doctor assured me she had been seeing a lot of this kind of illness lately, with days of vomiting instead of the usual 24 hours. She assured me that he was probably on the mend. And he was – he started to feel better that day, and completely better within two days. I breathed a deep sigh of relief. The overwhelming feelings of helplessness at a child's pain abated for the time being. And although his distress had been very real, my own reactions were largely made up in my head. I noticed this, and then let it all go.

DESIRE

We constantly want something. Attention, chocolate, quiet – lurking beneath our awareness are these little desires. Sometimes we can name them and meet the need. We can eat some chocolate or ask a friend for a hug. Often, however, these longings sit unacknowledged, controlling our behaviours and emotions without our even being aware of them.

A LL I'M ASKING FOR,' I lamented to my husband, 'is for my kids to eat, drink water, and sleep! I just don't think that's asking too much!'

I had just returned from the third post-bedtime call from a child: 'Mama!' shouted from the darkness of their bedrooms. 'I need water/my leg hurts/I feel dizzy/I can't sleep/the cat's in the room…' At dinner earlier, they had both poked at the food

and refused to eat. My son even started crying about how much he didn't want to eat dinner. Shortly before that, I had urged my daughter to drink more water after a long day at gymnastics camp. I promised she would feel better. But Mummy telling them to do something, even something as basic as eat/drink/sleep, causes my children to fight – picking, grumping, wide-eyed and freaked out.

I knew what every parent of a toddler knows. Take care of the physical basics first and then you can deal with just about anything. And also that whatever I want my children to do, they will fight. We know how resistant we ourselves can be to getting to bed on time and eating right. It's like some part of the human mind refuses to acquiesce to the body. It wants to force its power – I don't need to eat/drink/sleep. I am the all-powerful mind! And as a child, I am the all-powerful child who will not give up my power to any adult. Most especially not to my Mummy!

Power Play

So really what I wanted, I realized when I dug a bit beneath the surface, was for my children to give up some of that stubbornly held power to me. I wanted my schedule to be followed and my knowledge to be honoured. I wanted that feeling of smug satisfaction at the end of the day when both kids are in bed, asleep, and I get some time to myself. Time to 'be a grown-up'. Every parent knows that feeling.

There is nothing wrong with this feeling, nor with this power play. What trips us up, however, is that we don't notice that these desires to which we are so firmly attached are simply desires. We think the problem lies in our children being stubborn or not falling asleep or being picky at dinner. These are only problems when we make them problems. In fact, I turn my child's resistance to eating or difficulty winding down (despite all the things I've done!) into a long series of problems:

- He will be crabby tomorrow.
- She will call me again and I will have to get off my rump and go in.
- He will not get enough nutrition.
- She will get sick.
- I'm a failure as a mother because I can't solve this problem.
- I'm a failure and my children will grow up total complete messes because of it.

It's All in the Perception

It's almost funny to name the reactions my thinking mind goes through when I don't get what I want from my children. But mostly we don't name or become aware of these mental machinations, and we mistake them for reality. Or we think that they are problems. The problem is all in the perception.

Take 'He will be crabby tomorrow'. This is only a problem — even when it is true, and my child is rude and weepy when he hasn't had enough sleep – when I believe that my child should be happy and well-behaved at all times and that it reflects poorly on me as a parent when he is not. Whining is annoying. Tantrums are tiring. But the problem truly exists only in our thinking mind.

Often our immediate reactions are physical in nature. Studies have found that the most irritating noise possible to parents and non-parents alike is a whining child. But try it – next time your child is throwing a tantrum or whining, focus simply on what you see and hear. Notice your mind's resistance to the noise, the behaviour. What happens?

When we step out of the wanting – which starts with noticing it and accepting it without judgement – we can enter into authentic relationship. So first we notice – I want my child to honour my power as a parent so I feel effective in the world. It would be easy for me to feel ashamed of this desire. Or to feel self-righteous – damn sure I want that! The layers of feeling are simply more layers to be mindful of. Ah, look – I feel ashamed of my feeling this. Ah. Noticing. Eventually I am just noticing, just sitting right-now-here.

Right-Now-Here

Then a magical thing happens. I am right-now-here, and my child is right-now-here (even if she is actually throwing a tantrum), for that is the only place we ever can be. We can never be in tomorrow. We can never be in the past. Even the present is ungraspable and ever unfolding. You enter awareness of this space of unfolding, and then you exist in space and time with your child, and real relationship can happen.

Right now, as I write this, my son is shouting 'And-and-and-pee-pie-poop!' over and over and over. My immediate reaction is to tell him, 'Okay, enough!' because it's getting annoying and I'm trying to write! But since I am writing this, you remind me to be mindful and follow my own advice. I look down at him, present, witnessing, and I laugh. My self-importance and my irritation melt away.

He stops shouting and goes off to play.

TRANSFORMATION

As much as we resist and fear change, our lives are filled with myriad transformations. An infant grows into a child and then an adult. Ideally, we adults grow from green, overwhelmed parents into more solid, mature versions of ourselves.

I HELPED RAISE MY YOUNGER BROTHER. I had a subscription to a parenting magazine when I was thirteen. I babysat neighbours' children of all ages. I taught primary school. I learned infant massage and trained as a birth doula. One of my graduate programmes included classes in child development and developmental psychology. I read droves of natural parenting manuals.

I was prepared for this parenting gig like nothing else.

Then my daughter was born.

If you had peeked in the window on an average autumn day when she was but a few weeks old, you would have found me walking in circles, carrying a screaming infant facing forward because she insisted on facing forward. She is screaming. I am crying. My hair is unwashed, my shirt stained with leaking milk, my eyes smudged with big dark circles. 'I can't do this!' I remember saying. But of course I didn't really have a choice.

She cried a lot. I tried hard to respond to her cries by holding her all the time. I got good at holding or wearing her in a sling all the time. I cooked dinner facing sideways to keep her little body away from the heat. I had to move constantly while shopping – I literally had to jump up and down if I stopped to compare prices or choose a cut of meat or she would start screaming. She hated the car, where I could just get her to stop crying if I talked constantly; red lights made her cry no matter what. When I went to the loo, she sat on my lap. She woke up every two hours at night to nurse. She took at least half an hour of bouncing in my arms to fall asleep for any nap or bedtime. During the day she would nurse in little spurts. Her deep and all-consuming need overwhelmed me.

Victim or Spiritual Warrior?

I read so many books that said they had the solution. I refused to 'sleep train' her, and I felt strongly that breastfeeding on demand was important, but I was willing to do anything that fitted in the natural, attachment parenting model. Sleep solutions, bouncing, swaddling, getting hindmilk, gripe water, anything! Not much seemed to help. She was what they called a 'high-needs' baby. I learned later she has sensory processing issues, but when she was a baby, I did what I could to keep her happy, held, and moving. I was exhausted.

I alternated between feeling sorry for myself and framing the whole adventure as a spiritual challenge that would help me to grow.

Feeling sorry for myself is so much easier. It has this scab-poking comfort about it. I can feel self-righteously angry at... God? She sent me this impossible baby. Why me? Or mad at the baby. Or mad at the world that isn't actually a village helping me to raise her. Or mad at myself for being a colossal failure at the one thing that really matters.

But it gets old, being mad at everyone and everything, and wallowing about in a sludge of self-pity. When I'm stuck in victim mode I am weighted down by all the things I think others are putting on me. When I allow my feelings of 'stuckness' and frustration to simply be, and recognize them as my own feelings and reactions, my situation doesn't change at all. My exhaustion from waking up every two hours doesn't go away. But those daggers I'm sending at the world, at my husband, at my child, at God, they stop flying. I stop wasting energy on throwing them.

The Beginnings of Transformation

This isn't to say that I don't try to change things that I have the power to change. When I developed what might have been a bulging disc in my spine from bouncing the baby on an exercise ball to get her to go to sleep, and then this ball popped one day, dumping the two of us (unharmed) on the floor, I posted my conundrum on a forum for natural mamas. I learned about a baby bed that hangs on a spring. I found a friend who had one for sale locally. I bought it, despite our not having much extra money, and when I put my daughter in it and bounced her to sleep and she was out in seconds, I literally cried (silently) with joy and relief.

Two months later she learned to roll over in her bouncy sling bed and sit up, which meant she could fall out, and the great relief ended. I went back to bouncing her in my arms until she finally drifted off to sleep. (No more bouncy ball. I was afraid of it popping.)

I established a bedtime routine, one that we more or less follow to this day, nearly nine years later. I traded off with my husband. I lamented on my mama forum and then tried to let the feelings of frustration go.

And bit by bit a transformation took place. Not, at first, in my daughter (she didn't sleep through the night in her own bed until she was almost three), but in me.

I discovered that I could handle a lot more than I thought I could. Tired, yes, aching back, yes, crying baby, yes. I experienced all these things. But also I got some shapely calf muscles, some new mama friends, and a powerful bond with my little firecracker of a daughter. And all of it made me stronger.

One Breath at a Time

When my son was born, he didn't cry as much. He slept better. But as with my daughter, we got off to a rough start with breastfeeding (I thought I had that one down!), and I suffered from cracked, bleeding nipples and excruciating pain for at least six weeks. I still had to walk him around the dark house in the middle of the night to get him to sleep a few times. I got mastitis. Twice. My back ached from wearing him. But my daughter showed me that I have in me a core that is stronger than I thought, and that I could get through this even when all the books and salves and homeopathic remedies don't take away the hard stuff. When there isn't a choice, you show up because you have to. And because she taught me not to feel sorry for myself – at least not too much – I could show up with grace, taking responsibility for my reactions. One breath at a time.

This was my call – just as she called me to her again and again, I was called repeatedly to my warrior self. To my transformed, higher self. To the part of me that could rise to the challenge as it changes over time to be a 'good' parent and a 'good' person. That call is always there. Can you hear it? Where does it call you to follow?

CHAPTER TWO

MEETING YOURSELF

You have responded to the call and taken
steps along your Hero's Journey. Now you have a
chance to meet your greatest ally along your path:
your self. Discovering your true self is a path of
awakening. This journey, however, isn't always easy.
First we must face our shadows. We find these shadows
lurking in our 'darker' parts: anger, reactivity, striving,
judgements. Through the process of facing our shadows,
we ideally discover our true selves, our deeper
and more authentic identity.

ANGER

◆

Many parents I've spoken with agree that the flash of intense anger that can arise when struggling with their children scares them. Who is this angry, out-of-control person I have become? We tend to feel a lot of shame about anger, too. Can we perhaps learn from anger?

I'M STRUGGLING WITH ANGER TODAY. It is sitting beneath the surface like a swamp monster, gurgling and muttering to itself, ready to strike when someone steps too close. I witness the bitter tapes playing in my head: *Why doesn't he get the dirty laundry from our daughter's room? Does he not notice it? Is everything up to me to take care of? Okay, fine, don't listen to me. Why don't you put on a clean shirt and brush your damn hair?*

Noticing these grumbles, I bring my attention to my chest, where a tight ball of anger holds court. When I just observe, without judgement or comment, it unravels a little. I follow the string of sensation as it reveals sadness. Heaviness. Exhaustion. I become aware of a sense that no matter what I do, it's not enough. I will never get the house clean, never get the attention I long for, never reach a sense of safe arrival at wherever it is my ego has decided I need to be. I realize the anger is less a swamp monster and more an injured animal striking out at anyone and anything.

Strong emotions like anger can be a choice point. They can lead us deeper into the fighting, wounded ego, or we can use the emotion as a doorway into being more present and aware. Each time we choose the latter path, we grow and awaken just a little bit more. We deepen our compassion towards ourselves. This in turn allows us to deepen our compassion towards others, including our children. It teaches our children to honour their emotions and their needs and to learn how to ask for what they want in a mutually respectful way.

A Humbling Process

Beginning to really notice the grumbles in your head and the cranky emotions we frequently inhabit is a humbling process. We are all horribly judgemental, short, and cruel. Since we ask others not to be this way, it's really hard to notice how ugly we really are. I bet right now you're thinking, 'Well, she's talking about all those other people. I'm actually a really

---

Anger is energy – our personal jet fuel.
It is telling us that something needs adjustment in
our lives. It is telling us that there is something we want
that we don't know we want. Next time you get angry,
say, "Ah! My inner guidance is working. What is it I
want here? What do I want to have happen here?"
Anger is often an expression of the energy
required to make that adjustment.

---

nice, good person.' We really don't want to admit how cruel we can be. We don't want to admit it because our culture teaches us that it is shameful to be so. So we shove it all under the rug and desperately hope no one notices. Not least of all ourselves.

In the practice of Zen, however, we notice our shame just as we notice our anger and cruelty. It is just there. Once we notice without judgement something we might otherwise condemn, it loses its hold on us. We step out of the slime that coats our muck monster of shame/anger/not-enoughness, and exist not in the illusion of our mind, but enter the compassionate openness of what Buddhists call nirvana. Christians call it grace. It is a space of Beingness. You still exist, even as you expand into the vastness of open being, but no longer does the muck monster (or injured animal) control you.

Without our darker emotions like anger, we might just putter along blindly ensconced in our mind, never knowing the wider space of Being right-here-now. Anger and other challenging spaces help us to get to know our true nature. And why, you might ask, would I want to look into the eye of my own limitations and failures?

Because on the other side, you meet your truest self. The part of you that is part of God or the Tao or the Vast Mystery. This is the You that will carry you through this strange and fearsome life. The real You, that is always there, an ally along your journey.

PLAYTIME EXERCISE

SILLY ANGER

✳

Often we judge anger as unacceptable and bad, so we stifle it. But anger is there to be expressed — in a way that respects what you want and need while also respecting the feelings, boundaries and needs of the other person or people involved. One way to do this that works very well with young children is to be silly angry. You play up what you are feeling by putting on a little show: stomping, grimacing, and pretend yelling. This way you can communicate what you want, but make it a game. This only works when you recognize your anger and honour what it is telling you without judging. It also works best when it is a game of give and take, responding to your child's cues. The point isn't to frighten your child with how childlike you are, but to find ways to play with anger and speak needs and wants through play.

So you might respond to clothes dumped on the floor with 'AAAH! More clothes on the floor! They will some day take over the entire HOUSE!' using a silly voice. Use this tool playfully, not as a passive aggressive manipulation.

For more on this idea, see *Playful Parenting* by Lawrence J. Cohen, PhD.

DRAMA

◆

*We may roll our eyes at the angst-filled dramas of our pre-teen
children, but parents are not beyond their own overblown excite-
ments. We like being the centre of the universe. We enjoy the thrill of
feeling important. As soon as we are present and mindful, however,
the drama vanishes.*

I'VE BEEN REALLY BUSY LATELY. I am writing a book, taking
an online teacher licensing programme, doing my student
teaching hours at a home school enrichment programme,
working two part-time, sporadic jobs, dealing with a health
challenge, home schooling my children, and learning what it
means to have my daughter in a team sport requiring many
hours of practice, money, and commitment. I feel crabby and
overwhelmed and like quitting everything. I feel angry that
nothing seems to pay off, as we are dirt broke at the moment.
I'm annoyed with myself for scheduling a potluck at our
house for the community we've recently created around
backyard hen-keeping. I don't want to sit and write. I don't
want to be around people. I don't want to sit at home and
work while my husband takes the children to the beach. I just
don't want anything – I want to escape it all.

Remember new-mama me with my screaming infant? My
ego fought against this situation that demanded that I set aside
all I believed about myself and simply attended to my infant's

needs. I swooped in confidently – I will be the world's best parent! – and then fell apart when it got hard. I wanted to escape. It's the same thing now, and I recognize the pattern.

I'm up against my sense of importance – I didn't want to have to give up myself for my needy infant, and now, I don't want to give up my freedom to do whatever I want in order to satisfy the commitments I committed myself to. It doesn't matter that I chose all this – motherhood, writing, teaching, home schooling. Or even that I chose all these things in order to create a life that more fully expresses myself. It's all too hard, I whine, and my commitments are impinging on my freedom. I want to escape the hard place I've created and that the world has created for me.

We Need the Ego

Oh, the ego loves drama. The ego is a serious drama queen. It cannot see around the heavy make-up and flipped-over-the-shoulder hair, the diatribe about how slighted she has been, or the big huffy stomping up the stairs to her room. Because to her, these ideas about herself are reality. Without them, she doesn't exist. And not existing is the ego's greatest fear.

Now – I must make it clear that there is nothing wrong with the ego. We need our ego. In this incarnation, we need an identity. We need a place in the world, and we need a spine that helps us stand up to the overwhelming challenges of creating and keeping that place. I have chosen these commitments

because they express a piece of myself, and part of living this life is figuring out who I am and what that looks like. The problem happens – as does a whole lot of drama – when we so identify with our identity that we cannot see the grip she has on our larger self. When I get so wrapped up in my fears, perceived limitations, and whining about having to follow through on what I said I would do that I cannot move forward.

I stop whining. I ask myself – what is it that I am identifying with? What stories do I have in my head that are causing all this melodrama (aka suffering)? I'm so wrapped up in all of it that it takes me some effort to still my flurry of drama and just allow these messages to float to the surface. For underneath any drama or self-entitled suffering are ideas or stories we tell ourselves that give shape to what we think we need or deserve. 'I can't handle it all' comes up. Also, 'This isn't fun any more', which implies that every moment should be fun. And underneath is the surety that 'I am going to fail, so why try'.

As soon as these ideas arise, I see them for what they are. I can separate my feelings and reactions from them. Then I can choose what to do next, not motivated by these spinning fears and entitlements, but by what there is to do next.

What stories do I have in my head that are causing all this melodrama?

I Am Strong

I am feeling many of the same things now in regard to various situations in my life as I did when I had a screaming, needy infant. But then I did not have a choice to escape, not really. While career and partnerships and other life situations are ultimately escapable, parenthood is not. Yes, a person who is truly not equipped to raise children can choose to give them up. But for most people deciding to read this book, that isn't the case. It isn't for me. I would give up my limbs before I would give up my children.

That time with my new baby, as a new parent, taught me about being strong. I learned that I could endure far more than I thought I could, and that by taking things a moment at a time, I could get through it. Thrive, even. I got through that time, and I can keep recommitting to these moments, too.

So I write a sentence at a time. Show up to gymnastics meets. Go to the enrichment programme and have lovely moments with kids. Sleep a lot the next day. Home school my children. Ask for help where I need it, and do what needs to be done. Underneath it all, I notice – the stories, the fears, the crankiness. I do my best to let those pieces go, and to find the priceless moment that is gifted to me, moment after moment after moment. And when I let go of the drama, things have a way of working themselves out. When I let go of the drama, the joy that was there all along rises to the surface. I breathe, and it all has a way of working itself out.

CHASING THE FUTURE

◆

When we are over-identified with the mind, we don't even realize how much it skips ahead into the ungraspable idea of the future. We can begin to notice how much we identify with the mind, step out of its machinations, and use presence as a tool to live more joyfully.

I SPEND ALL DAY CHASING THE FUTURE. Before I even open my eyes, I think ahead to what I project this day will hold. Intentions, appointments, weather – they blip across my mind like waves on a heart monitor. Then breakfast, making sure everyone gets a balanced, protein-heavy meal, so that our moods in the future will be good ones. My husband goes off to work. I check the calendar. I check Facebook to see if any home-schooling friends are inviting us over or changing previously made plans. I check our shopping list and mentally tick off errands. I consider the weather as I load the children in the car with appropriate clothing (layers, hats, a change for this and that) and snacks for later. At the supermarket I plan future meals, birthday party needs, lunches, snacks – balancing healthy with what the children will eat. As we check out, I log the total in my budget, sometimes crossing my fingers that a cheque I wrote yesterday won't hit until pay day so this grocery trip doesn't draw money from our line of credit. I mentally tally any scattered income I have coming, hoping to inject new life into our dwindling funds on time.

On the way home, I plan lunch. I consider home school lessons we have waiting for us. I think of the week ahead, or of the weekend, going over plans. I bring things up with the children in the car so they are prepared, too, although I suspect that half of what I say is left on the back seat floor mats like biscuit crumbs.

Then it's unloading groceries, planning that night's dinner, maybe tossing things in the slow cooker. I check the clock; five hours until my daughter's gymnastics practice. I review with the children what they have eaten that day, then say yes, they can have a treat after lunch. We do some home schooling – I usually have to remind them that we are pleasant when we do school or I will find them a teacher. I wedge their learning into the file folder of their progress, both literally and mentally. Their overall curriculum is in my head. I know where we are headed, what they have learned so far, and what still needs to be done. I have filed away mentally a new thing to try next time when I can tell something isn't making sense.

When the kids are released for some free time on the computer, I spend a little time on the laptop, paying bills, checking emails, responding to birthday party invitations, and keeping up with my own work.

The mind of the future is ungraspable.

DIAMOND SUTRA [9]

As I drive my daughter to gymnastics, my son falls asleep in the back seat. I know that he will be up late because of it, but let him sleep. Then he wakes up and wants to go somewhere fun, like the bookshop. I think of what I have yet to do that day, and say not today. We inch back home in rush-hour traffic. I clean, read to him, cook. I check the clock to know when I have to pick my daughter up, or to note when my husband will be home to do so. I force myself to do a little yoga. I take my vitamins. I think about what else needs to be done.

Skipping Ahead

Planning and projecting keeps the motor of our home running smoothly. It's something I do well. But by the end of the day, I feel bored, unsatisfied and tired. When I let myself sit and notice, I become aware of how this always thinking ahead is like a drug, an addiction. My mind skips into this future space like my daughter's tongue pokes at the space where a tooth fell out. Thinking about what comes next gives me a frame to my day. A frame that sometimes, usually, feels like a cage. But it leaves me feeling important, indispensable. When I stop, however, I just feel drained, and it is never, ever enough to fully justify my existence and my choices and my self.

I have a recurring dream where I am on a bus but it never quite gets to my stop, or it goes a different way from how I expected, or it keeps going and going and I can never get home. That's what my obsessive mummy planning feels like.

In the dream I feel more and more panicky and unsure. In waking life, I try to stop, just breathe. I pride myself on being able to live in the moment, to develop awareness. In specific moments – birthing my children, a holiday feast, a moment in the garden – I remember to notice and honour the present. But I realize that in the invisible ongoingness of my life, in chores and planning and doing, I lose a sense of the sacred, the present, and awareness. Since life is mostly full of these mundane unfolding times, I need to find a way to become more mindful even then.

Moments of Mindfulness

I vow to create moments of mindfulness in the mundane mummy moments:

- Driving in traffic.
- Picking my daughter up from gymnastics.
- At random moments in the supermarket.
- While vacuuming, mopping, or taking out the rubbish.
- As I plan home schooling.
- While I wait for my son to fall asleep at night.
- Paying bills.
- Writing appointments on the calendar.
- And so on…

What are your mindfulness moments that can invite a space to breathe, stop and witness? How can you step out of the ungraspable mental addiction of living in the future? We can't stop planning, but perhaps, bit by bit, we can be present in our bodies as we do. Just thinking about it makes me breathe, relax, and welcome in more joy.

JUDGEMENT

◆

We rely on our brain's capacity to judge the value of sensations, information and choices. This valuable tool operates constantly and automatically. When our judging comes from a place of fear and inadequacy, however, it causes more harm than help.

IN ONE HAND, I'M HOLDING MY BABY. In the other, a full basket of dirty laundry. I'm hauling the laundry down the hall in an awkward sideways movement, determined to get it to the washing machine and get a load going. Halfway down the hall, it occurs to me to ask myself: 'Why does this matter so much? To whom am I trying to prove that I am "good enough" by doing "it all"?' Myself, I suppose. But also to the *idea* of the Perfect Mummy, which is sort of embodied by various things I've read and various women in my life with perfect houses and perfect physiques (these are not always the same women, I might mention) and internalized as this edict that I must somehow keep up with.

PLAYTIME EXERCISE

LIVE IN THE MOMENT

✻

Take some time today to interact with nature with your children, especially young children. Lie on your back and watch clouds pass over. Lie on your stomach and watch a bug amble past. Eat snow or catch snowflakes on your tongue. Try to catch a falling autumn leaf. Jump in puddles. Squish your hand in the mud. Be curious.

Try to live a few moments every day at a toddler's pace. How does your perspective change when you chop veggies for dinner, scoop up bubbles in the bath, or eat a strawberry from 'beginner's mind', as if you are experiencing something for the very first time? Indeed, you are experiencing it for the very first time, for nothing is ever exactly the same.

Judgment conquers our divine wholeness
and separates our inexpressible union into a dueling
dichotomy of incomplete parts.

KAREN MAEZEN MILLER[10]

This Perfect Mummy Ideal rears her rather ugly head when I observe other mothers, too. This is not something I happily admit, and as soon as I've had the thought, my more compassionate self squashes it. But, for that moment, I am thinking *Wow, she really needs to clean her worktops.* Or *That mother really needs a lesson on how to talk to her child.* Or *Maybe if she didn't feed her child artificial additives he wouldn't be such a pain.*

Like I said, I'm not proud of these thoughts. But they are there, sneaky and dark and the epitome of the judgement that conquers my divine wholeness. They are also human nature. We judge others, and ourselves, to keep ourselves safe and also to stroke the ego. The ego thrives on judgement, for it lives for black and white, good and bad, worthy and unworthy. These demarcations make sense to the ego, which seeks first and foremost to be safe.

I do not, however, have to live in this consciousness always. Judgement is a habit, as are most of the machinations we engage in to attempt to feel safe. By choosing mindfulness and an awareness of my knee-jerk reactions, I can slowly shift my habits towards compassion towards myself and others.

The Grasp of the Archetype

A big part of letting go of this kind of judgement for me is identifying the Perfect Mummy Ideal not just as an idea or an ideal, but as an archetype. An archetype isn't just an idea held in our minds, it also carries with it a sense of embodiment. We dream in archetypes. We fight wars for them. We build nations on archetypes. And when we believe that we must be able to meet that archetype on all levels, we are doomed to failure. It's not possible. While we might share certain aspects of ourselves with a given archetype, we cannot fully embody it. No one person can. When we realize that what we are comparing ourselves to is an archetype, and therefore impossible for any one person to completely embody, we can begin to let go of that internalized idea. We can begin to release ourselves from its grasp.

We dream in archetypes. We fight wars for them.

This freeing realization is true of any archetype. Men, for instance, compare themselves against the Provider Archetype or the Strong Man Archetype or the Sexiest Man Alive archetype – and inevitably fall short. Women tend to carry the idea that they have to be the Mother or the Lover or the Healer – or perhaps all three. There are many more – what archetypes do you compare yourself against? When you name it as an archetype, can you see how it is not actually possible for any one person to completely embody all parts of the ideal?

True forgiveness ... changes us at a core level.

It changes our bodies. It is an experience of grace.

CHRISTIANE NORTHRUP[11]

Forgiving Humanness

Realizing this frees us emotionally – I no longer have to be so perfect that I put my back out carrying the baby and the laundry. But it also frees and heals us physically. First, we will carry less stress in our bodies; stress is said to be the underlying cause of most, if not all, illness we encounter today. Second, we realize where we have held others in our lives against a given archetype, and seen them as letting us down, and we can begin to forgive them their humanness.

Rather than resenting the past or hating ourselves, we can be free to be who we are.

That Mother archetype (or Father or Healer or ...) we aspire to is just that – an archetype. Therefore, if our mothers or fathers fell a little short of that, or if we feel we are falling short, that is normal. So rather than resenting the past or hating ourselves, we can be free to be who we are. We can seek the healing we need to be whole, but we no longer need to hold the idea of healthy or whole against perfect. The archetype can then hold us, guide us, not cut us down or be a symbol of our failure.

Life is The Way It Is

Not only can we see how we are judging ourselves and others unfairly when we compare ourselves to an archetype, we can take it one step further and notice how the idea of the perfect life is something of an archetype. That's why when you start listing all the things about your life that you value, your life is actually pretty great, but it still feels like it falls short. You cannot name or put your finger on the amorphous thing that means a perfect life because it's an archetype. There is no way to figure it out. Life is the way it is. You can change some of the specifics sometimes, but not always. Part of mindfulness, and healthy, whole living, is giving up all those manoeuvres (sometimes literally, like me in the hallway with the laundry basket) and allowing life to be what it is in this moment, where I can finally notice that in this moment, nothing is lacking. Myself included. I can stop comparing myself against a societal pressure to be perfect.

We have to give up this idea in our heads
that somehow, if we could only just figure it out,
there's some way to have this perfect life that is just
right for us. Life is the way it is. And only when
we begin to give up those maneuvers does life
begin to be more satisfactory.

CHARLOTTE JOKO BECK [12]

IDENTITY

◆

Who are you? How do you define yourself to others, and to yourself? Without consciously thinking about it, you answer these questions many times a day. Your identity is a balancing act between your view of yourself and how you think others perceive you, between your authentic self and social belonging.

HOW WE ACHIEVE THE BALANCING ACT of identity affects how we parent, and how we see ourselves as parents. Subsequently, how we see ourselves as parents affects the crafting of our identity, or our idea of who we are.

In our type-A Western society, parenting has become a competitive sport that we think we have to excel at to be an okay person. We seem to regard our children as extensions of ourselves, proof that we are worthy people because our children are good kids, good students, good athletes. Many of us buy in to this cultural enmeshment (where our children are just extensions of ourselves) and this idea of kids-as-public-report-cards without even thinking about it. Why? I suspect that underneath is a fear that we are all failures. Perhaps a hangover from the strict religious past of Western civilization, we carry an idea that we are all supposed to be perfect. Parenting has become like a new religion. It used to be that we turned to religion to tell us who we are; today, many of us turn to our life tasks, including career and parenthood, to answer that question.

Children just used to be seen as part of life …

they were something you had, not something that

defined you. Now? They're like publicly available report

cards, documenting all our parenting successes and

failures. They embody our beliefs and who we are.

NANCY McDERMOTT [13]

Mirror, Mirror…

When we expect perfection, looking in the mirror is very uncomfortable. Our children (and often, too, our spouses, but that's a different book) are our mirrors. We see ourselves in them. We see our failures and dreams. We witness our bad habits replicated in miniature. We are shoved up against all the many ways we cannot help our children because we cannot control who they are. This highlights to us, at least unconsciously, how we cannot really control anything. And that is terrifying.

Try something. Sit in meditation for a moment, or just sit in noticing while you hold this book. Witness each of your senses. What is the sensation of sitting on the chair or lying on the sofa? What is the sensation of breathing in and out? What do you smell? What sounds reach your ears? With a soft focus, what do your eyes notice before you? What sensation of taste have you in your mouth?

Now – ask yourself, 'Who is aware?'

What part of you is aware of these sensations?

Yes, your nerves carry the information to your brain, and it processes and interprets the information. But there is a deeper or greater part of you that notices these sensations. You can even witness yourself noticing. What is that?

That is your greater self, your true self. It's kind of a paradox, because it's who you really are, and yet it is also known as No Self – your 'self' that is greater than yourself and in its expandedness, it is No Self. It's often called the Witness. Sit with that for a moment. What happens to your identity or sense of yourself?

Sitting With The Witness
As a parent, you are constantly getting messages from your children and the world telling you how you are doing and what you should be doing. You interpret these messages based on your ideas about yourself, your identity. Some of it – most of it – is unconscious, based on what you learned about the world from your parents. Some of it is conscious, like when you decide you aren't going to yell any more or you will be a better mother when you can get your child to school on time.

But how does it sit when the Witness (notice how that can be used as both a verb and a noun) observes your sense of your 'parent' identity?

Try this next time you are either triumphant or defeated about some parenting event. Something your children did or you didn't do. Witness what happens. Notice. Be aware. When you find yourself judging, just notice that. See what happens.

Here's an example. My daughter is at her gymnastics class. She can't do a certain skill that everyone else on her team can do. She's all disappointed in herself. I find myself being annoyed with her for being down on herself, puzzled at how to help her and her coaches achieve this skill, and annoyed with the coaches for not teaching her the skill well enough. I feel frustrated with everyone, and mostly with my own inability to control the universe and magically give her this skill. I don't want her to struggle and feel bad about herself.

When I notice my reaction to all this, I see that underlying the whole thing is my great love for my daughter, but also an idea that it is up to me to fix everything in my loved ones' lives. I see how I label parts of this situation as my own failure. I see, too, how hard it is for me to let her struggle and fail.

I don't tell myself I'm stupid for feeling this way, nor do I justify my reactions. They just are. When I witness them, though, I see how they are getting in the way of what just is. I cannot control the universe or my daughter or the coaches. And when I realize I was even trying to do so, and let it go, my shoulders relax. My child is just where she is. My identity as a mother is no longer tied up in her skill.

What happens when you witness your definition of yourself within the context of parenthood? How does that inform all other areas of your life?

CHAPTER THREE

ALLIES &
OBSTACLES

*On the Hero's Journey, the soul travels along
meeting allies and obstacles that move her forward
and teach her lessons. The hero's journey of parenting
offers us so many allies to help us on the road — and
ever so many obstacles, as well. Mindfulness and
compassion as states of being will help us along the
way as we discover that the destination is an ever-
shifting illusion, and that in the end, obstacles
often turn out to be allies in disguise.*

IMPERMANENCE

◆

Each micro-moment constantly unfolds into the next. Each breath is different. Each thought is new. Every experience is in some way different, even if our actions repeat. The slippery quality of change and impermanence can be frightening or refreshing, depending on our perspective of the moment.

A FRIEND'S TEENAGE STEP-SON was killed in a car accident two days ago. There is a part of me that wants to kick and scream and never let my children go anywhere. Another part of me feels jaded and blunt. I know far too well how impermanent this life is, and how young people die every day. I personally know friends who have lost babies; friends who died of various cancers before their twenty-fifth birthdays; friends and relatives killed in car accidents before their twentieth birthdays; and three young people who took their own lives. I know I could lose my own children or myself be killed by a thousand things before I am ready to leave this life.

It is this fear that haunts us when we become present to this ever-slipping-away moment. The present moment of this breath holds the raw reality of our own impermanence and the gripping knowledge that one day I will be separated from my most precious children. While I believe the soul lives on, I do not know that for sure. My mind clings to the possibility as well as rejecting it as irrational fluff.

By giving birth to two children, I invited into my life the possibility of these most precious lives being taken from me before their time. Furthermore, by inhabiting the impermanent present, I realize that 'before their time' is a construct, a clinging to happy illusion that just isn't real. It's an idea.

And yet, I cannot live each day in depressed fear. Fearing the future where my children might die in a car accident at any moment is just as unreal, just as ungraspable as living in denial that this could happen. It is just as much a mental construct as the idea that my children 'should' live a long, full life, or that my friends who died in their youth went before some time that should have been theirs.

All I can do in the face of these boggling mental dreams is to breathe.

All that really exists is right now, a moment for which I can be eternally grateful.

Becoming the Pain

Dharma teaches us that the root of all suffering is anger, fear and ignorance. When I am consumed with anger that a child could die and fear that my own children could die before their time, I am blinded with ignorance about my suffering. I allow the loss and the unfairness of life to run my thoughts. Which isn't to say that we can just shrug off the pain of loss – to do so would be as inauthentic as the idea that no one ever dies. Death is real. Pain is real.

In Buddhism, intense pain is dealt with by *becoming* the pain. Not fighting it, or denying it. The sorrow, confusion, anger, guilt – whatever is there, we allow it to be there, and we sit in it. We enter it, embody it. It feels like we will be lost inside it. But if we can truly stay present, we will not be lost. Instead, we will be found.

Those of us who fear entering the vastness of the present moment can learn from people who have faced this ultimate loss. All there is for a person to do here is to keep breathing, to sit in compassion. Compassion means 'to suffer with'. In the midst of blinding pain, we must sit in compassion with ourselves. We have to let whatever is there be there, without judgement, because what else can a person possibly do? We cannot escape the moment or the pain.

This Moment Is

Even as I go about my day, I try to come back to this central awareness. This moment is. I am. My children are. No matter if this moment is filled with pain or joy, it is this moment, and in the next moment, it will be gone. My heart swells with presence and gratitude for this simple gift of *this moment*.

Can you inhabit the impermanence of this moment? It can be a frightening place to be. We are reminded of the impermanence

Pain and suffering are both impermanent, though neither feels so.

of all we hold dear. That impermanence, though, is the secret to the universe. It is the secret to being free of your own suffering. Not of pain, but of suffering. Both are impermanent, though neither feels so. Suffering, though, can be gone in a moment, where pain may stay for ever. Notice your fear, anger, and suffering. Notice the moment slipping away. Be with that. Perhaps in time the obstacle of pain will transform itself into an ally; but for now, be with what arises.

ATTACHMENT

In child development, we talk about the importance of children's healthy attachments to adults. Another form of attachment, though, is our own mental rigidness about the world being a certain way. This form of attachment gets in our way of experiencing life as it is in the moment.

MY SON LOVES ANIMALS. He is especially enamoured with insects, and has captured a large, one-legged grasshopper. He feeds it fresh grass daily and watches it eat. It climbs the bug container desperately looking to escape. Next to One Leg lives an orange ladybeetle we discovered crawling on his ceiling one night. She has been given water, but we're short on aphids.

I discussed with him that it was okay to hang on to these bugs for a few days, but that we would have to let them go eventually, or they would die. I didn't mention that their life span isn't all that long to begin with. He got very sad. 'I don't want to let them go.' I said I understood. I acknowledged that he was taking such good care of them, but that they really needed to be in the wild, because they are wild animals. I told him the story of when I was little, his sister's age, how I used a fishing net to capture a bird as she flew out of a birdhouse. I kept her in my room under a laundry basket. I wanted a room lined with pets, but my only pet at that moment was a gerbil. My dog had recently been rehoused because he was too hard for my parents to care for (he was part Great Dane and untrained and very strong). I felt sorry for myself, the great animal lover, and I wanted to have this bird as a pet.

But then I watched her sit under the white plastic laundry basket, and I knew I had to let her go. The guilt was overwhelming me. So I carefully lifted her in my hands and let her out of the open window. As she flew off, I stared mournfully out at the summer evening and wished she could be my pet.

The story didn't help. My son still didn't want to let the bugs go. He is only five. And the sweet little guy is so full of love and want and passion for life, including bugs.

I'm left not knowing what lesson to teach him. That the bugs will die? That he will survive the grief of letting them go?

Notice the power
attachments have over us.

Or perhaps that we could keep them and feed them grass and aphids and then let them go just before it gets really cold so the ladybug can hibernate and the grasshopper can ... do whatever grasshoppers do in winter.

The Heart of Mindfulness

I realize that I'm just as attached to teaching my children the 'right' lessons as my son is to keeping bugs in his room. As easy as it is to justify either attachment, it's interesting to me to notice that they are just that — attachments to crafting the world a certain way.

Herein lies the heart of mindfulness. Noticing what we are attached to, and then noticing what choices we have. Often when we notice our attachments we are freed from habitual ways of being and the struggle that comes with them. We can be attached to so many things — emotions, things, certain future outcomes. The problem isn't really the attachment itself, it's not noticing the power it has over us.

Interestingly, as soon as I let go of the outcome and my attachment to getting the bug scenario 'right', he decided to let them go. 'I don't want them to die,' he said. As rain started to fall we opened the bug boxes. The big grasshopper stayed in his little box, and we decided to leave it for him, on its side, so he could stay out of the rain if he chose. My son deposited the ladybug in the garden, knowing it would soon hibernate. We proudly left the bugs to their lives and went inside.

PLAYTIME EXERCISE

THE SILENCE GAME

✳

Have you ever played the game in the car where you announce that everyone is playing the Silence Game, where the person who can be quiet the longest wins? The other evening we played it at dinner. I announced that we were playing a game to see who could be silent the longest – no talking. My five-year-old forgot and continued rambling on about his favourite Lego. My husband responded to my son. My daughter and I beamed conspiratorially at each other – we were winning! Then our smiles turned daring. Which of us would win? After a few minutes, I think she forgot we were playing. She spoke, and I shouted 'I win!' 'Let's play again!' she requested, determined to win.

The two of us (again the boys quickly turned to chatter) were totally silent for at least ten minutes. In that time, I noticed every time I wanted to speak. I caught myself wanting to butt in, correct, announce, control, plan, and spout off random thoughts.

Play the silent game with your kids. Notice what lies behind your urges to speak. Notice what you are attached to, and let this wisdom become an ally on your journey.

IMPERFECTION

◆

We hold ourselves against perfect ideals — the house ready for a magazine photo shoot, our children looking (and behaving) as if they were in a catalogue for expensive clothing, ourselves calmly eligible for the Super Parent of the Year contest. Then when we fall short, we feel deficient, harried, and exhausted.

PART OF MINDFULNESS PRACTICE is recognizing and accepting that life is imperfect. When we accept this fact, our shoulders can relax a little. We can breathe a little deeper, for no longer are we running from the Perfection Police. Our children can relax, too, for we stop fixing their hair, tucking in their shirt labels, and frowning at the chocolate on their faces. We let kids be kids, ourselves be human.

When we are no longer trying to erase all imperfections as if they advertised to the world how screwed up we really are, but allow imperfection and messiness to be a part of life, we can then enter a space of learning and growing from imperfection. We stop pretending that life can be perfect, stop striving for this perfection, and follow imperfection to enlightenment. Again, Suzuki Roshi said, 'In your very imperfections you will find the basis for your firm way-seeking mind.'[14] By going in to our imperfections, we find our way. We discover who we are. We find wholeness and healing. We transform obstacles into allies.

Naming the Sensations

My daughter struggles with anxiety. This comes up most strongly when we are preparing to leave for her gymnastics practice. She is worried that we will be late. She tenses, makes a high-pitched whining noise, stares at the clock, pointing at it in horror, and bouncing up and down. I have tried reassuring her by naming and affirming her concerns: 'You are worried we'll be late. We will be on time. Trust me.' I try making jokes: 'What will happen if you are late? Will your coach put you on her shoulders and run around the floor yelling, "She was late!"?' Despite herself, she smiles, but the anxiety still holds court. Sometimes these strategies help; mostly they do not.

Finally, one day on our way to practice, slowly inching along in traffic, I asked her to close her eyes and breathe into the spot that feels afraid. She did. I asked her where it was located. She put her hand over her low belly. As someone prone to anxiety myself, and also an empath, I knew exactly what she was feeling. We named it: 'You feel tight and scared in your low belly,' I said. She nodded. Then I asked, 'What

---

Only by tuning in to how

we feel in our bodies can we appreciate

our inner guidance.

Christiane Northrup [15]

---

does it mean to be late?' She couldn't answer that. I sat in that feeling, open, not analysing, just letting that idea of 'being late' speak to me. Waiting with it to reveal something to me.

What Is This Really About?

The idea came into my mind that people who are chronically late are often unconsciously trying to control the situation. The idea of control came up. I asked my daughter, 'Do you feel anxious because you cannot control the traffic, and you cannot control when I leave?' Aha! She nodded, and her body relaxed just a little. 'When you arrive late you feel out of control.' She nodded again. The anxiety wasn't really even about being late, it was about not feeling in control. Once we were able to figure out the real feeling, we could name it. Then we could name what she really wanted: 'You want to feel in control of when you arrive. You want to feel in control of yourself at the beginning of practice.'

The next time she began to feel anxious about the time, I named again what she wanted: 'You want to feel in control of leaving and arriving on time.' Her anxiety lessened by at least half simply by stating this want.

When I had been trying to erase the imperfection by making my child behave herself and trust me, we got nowhere. But when I allowed the imperfection – the struggle, the anxiety, the fear – to speak to us, we found our way, or at least the beginnings of our way-seeking.

Feel It Fully

I recommend this practice in yourself and your children whenever you encounter an area of challenge. You may have to help your children through this practice, as they often cannot name what they really feel and want (some kids are great at this, others not so much – either way is okay). Here is the process:

1. Acknowledge what you are feeling fully, without judgement. Feel it fully.

2. Acknowledge that you are feeling this way for a reason.

3. Spend twenty seconds or so identifying why you are feeling this way. Sometimes this will take longer, but the point is not to dig and wallow, but to identify. Mindful body awareness is a useful way to find out what is bothering you if you cannot immediately identify why.

4. Identify what you *do* want. This is probably the opposite of why you feel the way you do. (I feel out of control, I want to feel in control.)

5. State clearly what you want.

6. Affirm that you have the power via your inner guidance and power of intent to get what you want.[16]

The first step to identifying what you want is to feel the 'imperfection'. It is through this that you find your way. This process works for huge issues, like needing to change jobs, and for little things like wanting your family to pick their dirty socks off the floor. Doing this practice regularly will bring you clarity, clear out resentment, help you deal with challenges, and develop in you and your children a deeper compassion for yourself and others. It will help you identify what steps you need to take to get what you want and need to feel whole. Accepting that life is imperfect and then listening to that imperfection or your suffering about it will lead you to live your most healthy and joyful life.

EFFORTING

◆

When faced with the feeling of Not Being Enough, we either shut down or push on through with dogged determination. This latter response I call Efforting. We push and effort our way towards Being Enough. We will never get there; there is always more to prove in this losing game.

JUST AFTER I WEANED MY SON, I experienced what I call an adrenal crash. When the adrenals are fatigued, there just isn't enough energy to go around, and I had to learn to conserve. So I began noticing places where I was using way more energy or effort than I needed to. I would be performing some mundane task with the effort of a mountain climber seeking a summit. I would find myself racing to get all the laundry in the washing machine and then dashing about with the vacuum when there was nowhere I had to rush off to, no inquisitorial committee peering over my shoulder. I would notice how tensely I held my body as I paid bills or sorted my children's clothes. I asked myself — *why am I working so extra hard here? It is as if I am trying to prove something to someone.* Which of course is exactly what I was doing. Unconsciously I had this belief that I needed to prove to the world, my parents, my husband, my children, the Great Super Mum in the Sky, that I am doing a good job. I am good *enough*.

We try so hard to be perfect. As a parent, I seek the best ways to raise my children, and when I fall short I work to fix what I can. I know I'm far from perfect, though. Given this, I have two choices. I can beat myself up and exhaust myself trying ever harder — what I call efforting — or I can notice the places I strive and the places I fail and hold it all with gentle compassion. The way to do this is simply to accept what is. Change may grow from that point, but the first step is to stop efforting all the time in every little thing.

One of the most powerful teachings
of the Buddhist tradition is that as long as you
are wishing for things to change, they never will.
As long as you're wanting yourself to get better, you
won't. As long as you have an orientation toward
the future, you can never just relax into what
you already have or already are.

PEMA CHÖDRÖN[17]

The Ego is a Toddler

We have to approach our egos, which strive and effort to make things better, like a toddler having a tantrum. Usually we try to make them stop. We offer bribes, shame them, threaten with punishment, but of course nothing works. But have you ever just sat and let them freak out? You might give them a pillow so they don't hit their head on the hard floor, but mostly you just sit and breathe and hold the space. You let them know by not reacting that they are okay, even in the midst of all their turmoil. And what happens? They eventually calm down. Sometimes they even forget why they were so mad in the first place. Your ego is a toddler. It wants, wants, wants – it thinks that if you just do this and that, everything will fall into place. It really believes that there is a 'someday' when life will be perfect and you'll have it all together.

Have you ever gained that point? Known anyone who has? Where everything is truly perfect on all accounts? (I mean besides on Facebook.) No, because it doesn't happen. That's not a part of this flawed and crazy life. I bet, however, that you have had little glimmers, little moments, where everything feels right. It has nothing to do with making it just so, and everything to do with being centred in this moment, letting what is just be. Sort of like the toddler who awakens from her tantrum and sits in that still peace of release. She comes to reside in a place where it is no longer about *enough* or *not enough*. It is just this moment, this sensation. Or those moments when you feel at peace, which are never about having everything in life figured out. Those moments are found only when we step outside of the chattering, judging mind, and into present sensing.

Noticing when you are efforting – pushing to be good enough, pushing to achieve it all and have it all together – will free you from the tantruming, grasping ego. Just for a moment. Then you find that space where you can slow down and let go, where you can allow the present to unfold as it is and find the peace waiting for you there. That beautiful peace is one of the greatest allies on your Hero's Journey.

THINGS

◆

We exist in a material world. Often the stuff of the material world entices us into believing that security and power come from posses-sions. Sometimes the inverse happens, where we believe that we are better by our asceticism. Both are imbalanced perceptions.

M Y SON IS A COLLECTOR. We have two baskets filled to the top with wooden trains and their tracks. A bucket of cars. A basket of Pokémon figures and a few trading cards. Two clear plastic tubs of Lego. A basket of little animals and plastic bugs. Another container of superhero action figures. We are a home-schooling family, so when my children get into something, we explore it in as many ways as we can.

We order books from the library, check out any pertinent websites and shows, and we collect the play figures. But then, when he has moved on, he really, really doesn't want to get rid of any of those toys.

I don't really fault him here, for wanting things and equating having things with security and power is a pretty human thing to do. I probably wouldn't really notice it at all except that we have a very small house, and the toys pile up and fall over into the hallway before we know it. So we have clearing out days a few times a year. Because if there is any-thing I like more than buying things, it's getting rid of them. It becomes a practice in letting go, in sharing with others, and in non-attachment.

Then I triumphantly take a bag of toys and clothes and whatever else (we grown-ups have to clear out stuff, too) to the thrift store or the consignment store.

The Meaning Behind

From a mindfulness perspective, the problem isn't the things themselves, nor is it having lots of things. The problem is that we equate a sense of okayness — goodness, even — with these *things*. The nature of the ever-unfolding universe is that every-thing changes. All things eventually die away. Except for the Tao, or God, or Love. Underneath this longing sits that Eter-nal Infinite Energy. It is the only thing that can begin to fill that pit of longing.

Ironically, rejecting materialism gets us into almost the exact same boat as attachment to things does. Suddenly we are attached not to the things we rejected, but to the ideal of asceticism. We lose ourselves in one ideal or the other.

When we become present, we encounter the Energy beneath everything, and from that awareness arises a para-doxical sense – all is ephemeral, and all is sacred. Material things then become either nothing, easy to release, or repre-senting and leading us to the sacred.

My son's passion for collecting things is a normal pastime for a five-year-old. My desire to have a nice home and garden is a normal part of being a mother in my culture. We are both learning, though, how the meaning behind something is so much more important than the thing itself. I am learning, too, that the meaning is something I create and give power to. I am learning that there is nothing wrong with any of these rela-tionships to things as long as I understand they are relationships and ideas that I as a material human have created. Indeed, sometimes they help me stay rooted to this present moment. Sometimes, though, it is not the thing I need to hold on to, but the feeling, and feelings take up little shelf space.

My desire to have a nice home and garden is a normal part of being a mother in my culture.

PLAYTIME EXERCISE

CREATE A FAMILY TREASURY

As a family, create a space to collect family treasures and honour the essence of home. This space is like a family altar mixed with a gallery, a treasury of objects that hold memories and energy of your unique family. It is a space to pause and be present to all that makes your family special. Choose a visible and central location. A mantle, the top of a deep shelf, or a side table not used for anything else. Place items on the treasury in a mindful way. Include treasures gathered on nature walks, such as pine cones and shells. Include items that represent the spiritual traditions your family follows. Let the space change with the seasons by including such things as autumn leaves and pumpkins, or flowers. Honour activities, events and holidays with souvenirs, seasonal decorations and crafts. Pictures of loved ones or ancestors might be a part of your treasury. As life moves forward, replace old items with new ones and either discard or tuck away what you have removed. Include some safe candles and use this family-centred sacred space to meditate or calm down. You might end the day with a little ritual of giving thanks, or create new family rituals that help you honour the meaning of home.

CHAPTER FOUR

FINDING THE STILLNESS

Our obstacles and allies have led us here,
to this space of presence. Inside our awareness,
protected from the business of life, is a pool of stillness.
We can only get there by letting go of all efforting.
As soon as we try to relax, we aren't relaxing! In order
to find the stillness, we must stop pushing ourselves
to achieve something and let the stillness find us.
This is the part of our journey where we begin
to find our true selves.

EXPERIENCING

◆

Come into this present moment by tuning in to your own sensory experience. Keep coming back to the now. This is the heart of mindfulness. One place to begin is with your breath. Focusing on the sensation of breathing brings you into your experience.

'TAKE A DEEP BREATH,' I tell my daughter, now eight years old. She executes a tight, quick, in-out breath and continues to curl up in a ball. I take my own deep breath, mostly in an attempt to release my own spreading irritation.

'That's not a deep breath.' I put my hand on her stomach. 'Can you breathe in enough to push up my hand?' She tries, sort of, but her shoulders lift in tight little daggers towards her ears. Under my hand I feel taut tummy muscles as a teeny poof of breath pushes outwards. 'Come on, breathe dooooooown,' I say, lowering and stretching out my voice. 'Down into your belly, down into your hips.'

It's like she is trying to inflate a turtle shell. I try a different tactic to get her to relax.

'Can you feel the angry inside you?' I ask. From her tight ball of resistance she gives a teensy nod. 'Where is it?'

Where the Angry Sits
She's played this game with me before. I can tell she wants to resist noticing as much as she resisted taking a deep breath.

She knows that noticing and naming will lead her to let go a little, and she's hanging on to this anger like a life raft.

'Chest,' she says in a quiet, clipped voice.

'The angry is in your chest,' I say back to her. She gives another tiny nod. And despite her clinging, her tight ball opens and softens just a tiny bit.

'Where else?' I ask.

She notices for a moment, curiosity getting the better of her righteous anger. She gestures furtively to her jaw. I nod. My own irritation has dissipated, I notice. Instead of trying to get her to do something – relax, chill out, and breathe – I am inviting her into her own space of body awareness.

'Okay,' I say. 'You notice angry in your chest and tight jaw. And maybe your tummy,' I suggest, because I can feel the tension there, too. 'What happens when you look at that sensation? Just feel it, look at it, listen to it.'

Tears bead in her eyes.

'Ah, up comes some sadness,' I say. She dissolves into sobs. I hold back my eye rolling and take another deep breath of my own. Her melodrama triggers me. I try to do what I am inviting her to do, and just notice my own resistance and tension.

'Where does that sadness live in you?' I ask. I know that while the tears are genuine, the dramatic sobs grow from her feeling sorry for herself.

The sobbing abates a little as curiosity peeks in. She points to her chest again. 'The sad lives in your chest, too. Sad that

it's hard to communicate sometimes. That you were trying to help your brother and he didn't want your help?' She nods.

Just Notice…

The reason we are sitting here on the floor in a tight ball of sorrow, by the way, is that her brother didn't want her to tell him how to play a computer game. My daughter really really likes being helpful. Even when the other person doesn't want any help. When her helping is rejected, she takes it as a threat to her very identity and place in the world. First she gets door-slamming mad, and then she buries herself in blankets and sobs, saying things like 'Everybody hates me' and 'I wish I didn't exist'.

Now, these are phrases that in a less adjusted person might indicate serious problems. My daughter is, however, a healthy kid with the normal ups and downs of the seven-to-nine-year-old girl. Often, when she falls into this pit of despair, I realize that she is just voicing something that I, and my husband, and probably lots of other adults, sometimes feel but don't voice. We adults have mostly learned to shove these feelings of melodramatic worthlessness under an internal rug, buck up, and sally forth.

However, neither melting down into end-of-the-world sobs nor shoving it all under the rug accomplishes much of anything. What both children and adults need to learn is just to notice. When we notice what is there, we can release all the

chatter about what happened. We notice the angry feeling, and the sad. We notice the little phrases zinging through our minds: 'No one loves me – I'm worthless – no one trusts me – he must hate me – etc, etc, etc' – and see how our ego feels bruised. Then we can take responsibility for what we are ourselves feeling, and 'use our words' (to utilize the oft-repeated phrase of parenthood) to communicate with those around us.

Very simple – but not always easy.

Become Present to What Is

Experiencing what is in the present moment requires that we develop new habits. We are all so used to avoiding responsibility for uncomfortable feelings and the behaviours they inspire. Anything that is uncomfortable is obviously someone else's fault, we like to believe. We like to blame and find fault, either with others or with ourselves. Experiencing and taking responsibility is not about fault, however. It is about being present to what is, and releasing judgement.

A strange thing happens when you become present. You do what there is to do. You drop a glass and it shatters. You notice the shattered glass, and then you pick up the pieces. Your child cries about not getting a toy. You hold him and let him cry. The petrol light comes on in your car. You stop at the nearest petrol station. What is there to be done is there. We can see this when we experience what is. And when you do this, you teach your children how to as well.

PLAYTIME EXERCISE

WHAT COLOUR IS YOUR FEELING?

This activity can be done spontaneously when someone is struggling with an overpowering feeling, or as a planned activity. Emotions and feelings are physical sensations that reside in our bodies. Noticing those sensations can help us to be less overwhelmed by or controlled by our feelings and less identified with them.

Sit or lie down in a comfortable position (this can be done in any position, like my daughter's tight ball, but when you are comfortable you can more easily notice areas of tension). Take a few breaths. Notice whatever sensations you experience right now. Notice where these sensations live in your body. Do these sensations relate to an emotion? Feel it. Breathe with it. If it's hard to pay attention to a sensation, just gently invite your attention back to that area. Does your sensation/emotion have a colour? A texture? A shape?

Talk about the sensations, or colour a drawing of your experience. Notice how your relationship to the sensation or emotion changes simply by your being present to it.

The next time my son rejected my daughter's help, she got mad. And the next time. But one time, a few days later, he said no, and she walked away and did something else. I smiled at her and gave her a hug. She smiled sheepishly back, and went on with what she was doing.

ATTENTION

Where is your attention focused? On your thoughts? On the future or the past? On your fears? Bring your attention to the moment, to sensation. From there, you have greater choice about where to direct your attention, rather than being lost in the spiralling mind.

IT'S THE START OF THE HOLIDAY SEASON; Thanksgiving (in the us) is a few days away. I have pledged this year to do only what I want to. I will bake only if and when I feel like it. Shopping for gifts will not be about coupons and deals, but about locally owned small businesses and things or experiences that will be cherished by the recipient. My husband and I discussed the upcoming family gift-giving among adults, and decided that we would vote for time spent together and not the exchange of things. Some of our family members might not love this idea. But I want simple, and I know the other mother in our extended family with small children agrees. Our kids have plenty of stuff. We adults have plenty of stuff. What we really all long for is experiences: playing in the

We in our affluent society put a lot of pomp and circumstance into the holidays in an attempt to create cherished memories.

snow, decorating the tree, sipping hot chocolate, skating around the kitchen in woolly socks.

I think we in our affluent society put a lot of pomp and circumstance into the holidays in an attempt to create cherished memories. We want it to be perfect, partly because we hold ourselves to creating the archetype of the holidays (just like the archetype of the Perfect Mother), but also because we want ourselves and our children to have – and remember – the best Thanksgiving/Winter Solstice/Christmas ever. We know, as parents, how fleeting life is. We want the glow and joy to last for ever.

The way to create moments like this, however, is not to scramble about making everything look perfect. Quite the opposite. The secret to creating the 'perfect' memories is to be present. To experience each moment with mindfulness.

Cherished Moments of Mindfulness

Think back on special moments of your life. Holding your newborn, getting married, watching a sunset, hugging a cherished friend. Take yourself back to that moment. When you were experiencing that moment, were you mentally else-

where? Or were you fully living that one moment? I am guessing that your senses were fully engaged with whatever you were doing, at least for a moment. When you hold a newborn, your brain shorts out on his perfect skin and that overwhelming baby smell. The moments you remember from your wedding were moments when you blocked out all the mind chatter and focused on this moment with your beloved. And often – though of course not always – the memories you cherish from holidays past were events that were unplanned. Like when my daughter got a pair of roller skates and my son a glider bike, and since our hardwood floors are ancient and ratty, we just rolled back the carpets and allowed them to ride and skate in circles around our little house. Or one of my favourite memories from when I was in college, and my parents and I went for a walk on Christmas Eve in the dark, through the snow. I remember when I was about twelve, my brother and I turned off all the living room lights and lay beneath the lit Christmas tree with our stuffed animals.

I do remember special gifts: a book I still have, a Barbie dining room set that I played with for years, a bear I got when I was three who still sits beside my bed. Gifts are certainly a

◆

But what our children really need is for
their mothers [and fathers] to be present with them.

NANCY HATHAWAY [18]

◆

part of the season, but they can be either cherished moments of mindfulness or the mindless overwhelm of consumerism. It is up to you to make that choice.

Pay Attention to Your Inner Calm

A side effect, if you will, of being present during the holiday season is that you will feel so much calmer. When this moment matters more than the chaos, you sit in a pool of stillness in the middle of the craziness. When you are in the middle of a busy shopping centre, in the midst of baking three pies and five dozen cookies, or rushing to your child's holiday play, if you take a moment to tune in to your inner stillness, you will relax just enough. Your breath deepens. Your shoulders let go. The simple joy of existing in the moment sneaks in.

Our brains process millions of bits of information each moment. We don't notice most of it. If we did, we would go insane. Mostly this filtering happens unconsciously, like breathing. But like breathing, we can also do it consciously. When we choose to pay attention to our inner calm, to our breath or our senses, our brain can relax a little. We can stop trying to take in all the chaos, and just be present.

Stay in the center of your own soul.

There is nothing else you can do.

WILLIAM MARTIN [19]

PLAYTIME EXERCISE

SOUND GAME

Discuss how focusing on something really hard can reveal new information. It can also help us to become present. If your children are into superheroes, you might want to present this game as Super Hearing. Play a sound that resonates and then goes quiet, like a gong, piano key, or Tibetan tingsha. Tell your children to listen very very carefully, turning on that Super Hearing, and then to raise their hand when they stop hearing the noise. Try this a few times. Discuss the experience and how they feel while doing it. When we totally tune in to our senses, we become present in this moment. Think of ways you can play this with other senses, too: stroking a cat slowly, with your eyes closed; tasting a strawberry; looking at a leaf under a microscope. In what other ways can you play with being fully present?

NO-SELF

◆

As you meditate, your mind slowly quiets. Simultaneously, you settle into a sense of being no longer identified with your mind. You settle into the pool inside you, through you, around you. You become your most true self, and also beyond yourself as well. This is sometimes called the No-Self.

THIS IS THE PRACTICE OF MINDFULNESS, to come into the centre of the moment where those problems melt away, and suddenly we are connected – indeed, *interconnected* – with all Beingness. All the words I write, the parts of noticing, the tools of the journey, they are then a part of the whole of what is. It is not an easy practice, nor does it happen immediately. However, we can all feel a piece of this centredness in little moments of any mindfulness practice, and over time these moments add up.

So much of parenting today is about ego. When we are triggered by our sassy nine-year-old or the toddler who won't put on his shoes, it is because we are living from our ego space. We are attached to a certain outcome, a certain response. When we feel guilty because we don't spend 'enough' time with one child or because we contributed store-bought treats to the bake sale, we are living in our egos. Getting angry at the parent who suggests we are wrong to vaccinate, not vaccinate, home school, school, discuss current

events, or not discuss current events with our children – that anger comes from the ego. There is nothing wrong with this. It simply is. We have an ego, and we usually respond from that space of self-centredness, fear and reaction.

However, mindfulness practice can take us out of this fear and ego into a place of No-Self. We settle into stillness from which action can arise not from reaction but from natural flow. This is because we finally see through the jumble of thoughts always clattering about in our minds, and then what needs to be done can be seen clearly. Our lives – or at least moments of

As you meditate… you become your most true self, and also beyond yourself as well.

them – become calm pools instead of choppy waters, through which we can see what steps we need to take to get to the other side.

Benefits of Mindfulness

Centredness helps us as parents. It also affects every area of our lives. The transformation happens slowly, but you will notice over time you will react less to rude drivers, long queues, and snarky partners. This transformation is what meditation and mindfulness is all about – not merely relaxation, but a settledness into your centre that leads to all sorts of outcomes, including relaxation, improved attention and overall better health.

Inhabiting the place of No-Self or centredness can lead to many more surprising results. In one study, a Buddhist monk who had practised meditation for over forty years was able to nearly eliminate his automatic startle response while practising 'open presence meditation'.[20] Meditation practice is shown to lower amygdala response to negative situations (the amygdala is the part of the brain responsible for stress responses, which labels something a threat or not).[21] When we practise mindfulness, it literally changes our brains. It changes our blood pressure and our perception of pain. Draw on this knowledge when you find yourself overwhelmed by anger. Before you yell at the kids, take a deep, mindful breath. You will literally change how your brain responds to the challenging situation, and in doing so, change your reaction.

Meditation also leads to greater personal growth. Ken Wilber writes, 'In short, the more one *goes within*, the more one *goes beyond*, and the more one can thus embrace a *deeper identity* with a *wider perspective*.' [ital. in original][22] Interestingly, that is what many parents hope for their children, that they would grow enough to embrace a deeper identity with a wider perspective. Again, we see how a practice of mindfulness helps us to be better parents and more whole ourselves.

Centredness helps us as parents...
and affects every area of our lives.

COMMITMENT

◆

To commit is literally to put something with something else by pledging or through obligation. So many of our commitments are unconscious, but like an explicit commitment, they dictate our actions. What have we pledged ourselves to without even realizing?

WHEN I FIND MYSELF BEING IMPATIENT or angry with my children, I try to notice what assumptions underlie my reactions. Why am I so impatient? So angry? What buttons are being pushed? In any given moment we are unconsciously (sometimes consciously) committing to a vast set of assumptions about ourselves, the world, and those with whom we interact. We carry beliefs about ourselves and the way things work that underlie our actions. When our behaviour doesn't line up with what we *think* we are committing to, we need to dig a little and uncover what lies beneath.

I use the word 'commitment' here because that is what we are doing: committing ourselves to an idea or set of ideas. Usually we think of ourselves as committing to something big, like a religious practice, a new diet, or a responsibility. We commit to thousands of 'small' things in each moment, as well, without even thinking about it. Take, for example, a household chore. I might whine that I really don't feel like vacuuming. I feel tired and it sounds boring and it will take too long and checking Facebook again sounds so much more

engaging. But then I decide that I do want the floor to be clean, so I haul out the vacuum and begin. I rarely feel the same angst I did before beginning my task. Once I have committed to doing the task at hand, my resistance melts away. I have committed to the task, but also to the idea of whatever it is that I am doing.

What Am I Committed To?

When we are headed out the door to go somewhere and my children are moving slowly and I find myself irritated with them, I try to stop myself and notice: what idea am I committed to here? What belief underlies my actions and reactions? I have a whole host of ideas to draw from; I might commit to the idea that my time is more valuable than theirs, or that other people will be annoyed with us if we are late. I might believe that it's really important to keep moving so that I feel like things are being accomplished. I might be committed to an idea that I am the person of power and my needs and desires should be carried out by my children. If I unconsciously believe any of these ideas, I will be impatient and snippy with my slow-moving children.

However, if I stop and notice these underlying ideas, I will no doubt decide that these are not ideas I actually want to be motivated by. What I really believe is that my children are the most important people in the world to me. That we will get there when we get there. That some things require being on

time, so we leave early enough to do so, and other activities are more time flexible. I believe that children who are respected as individuals grow up to respect themselves and others, and have an easier time figuring out what they want out of life. I also believe in speaking to my children and others with respect, and teaching them to do the same.

When I notice that I am acting from the first set of beliefs and not the second, I stop, take a deep breath, and recommit to what I really believe. Then I am able to identify what needs to happen and respectfully let my children know that. 'I need everyone to get in the car now so we will be on time to meet our friends.' Most of the time, unless there is a problem that needs addressing more immediately (like, say, a lost sock), my children respect what I have said. Whereas when I just crabbily snap at them to *get in the car already*, we all set out on our adventure in sour moods. My reaction to internal ideas trickles down to affect everyone, whether I like it or not.

Clearing the Air
A sour mood is often a sign that we are committing to some belief that doesn't serve us or our loved ones. Looking at what that assumption is doesn't always feel comfortable. I don't like

What I really believe is that my children are the most important people in the world to me.

discovering ways in which I am being selfish, judgemental or rude. My ego likes to give all sorts of justification for why I am behaving inappropriately. I find, though, that when I am honest with myself and my children (or whomever I am dealing with), the air clears. We can all take a deep breath. Change and growth can happen, and we are all better for it. Also, I find I can understand better the motivations behind my children's less-than-ideal behaviours. When I can name them, gently, we can try to solve underlying issues rather than gridlocking in blame and shame.

These underlying beliefs often lead us to even bigger assumptions and commitments. If I am acting out of a commitment to the idea that I need to be productive all the time, I need to ask myself what underlies *that* belief. We often need help uncovering and healing from these unconscious destructive beliefs in the form of therapy, journaling and spiritual practice. We all carry self-destructive beliefs of one variety or another. Taking the journey of uncovering these beliefs and healing them is the definition of personal growth, and it leads to a healthier life for ourselves and our children.

The Eight-fold Path

One of the teachings of the Buddha is called the Eight-fold Path. It teaches that to be healthy and balanced, we need to live 'right' truths in all areas of our lives, including:

1. *Right Understanding* – Understanding that all things are interconnected, so we must do no harm.

2. *Right Thought* – Thinking that grows from Right Understanding.

3. *Right Speech* – Speech that grows from Right Understanding and Right Thought.

4. *Right Action* – Behaviours and actions that arise from Right Understanding.

5. *Right Livelihood* – Earning a living in a way that causes no harm.

6. *Right Effort* – Balanced effort.

7. *Right Mindfulness* – Practising awareness.

8. *Right Concentration* – Balanced attention on Right Understanding.

'Right' in this case is defined as ethical, disciplined and wise, and arising from the underlying foundation that all is interconnected, all is part of an interconnected field of Being-ness, and we must strive to do no harm. I bring up this idea here not to get dogmatic, but because it names all the areas of our lives that need examining. When we bring our own lives back into alignment with Right Living, we heal ourselves while setting a positive example for our children.

COMPASSION

◆

When we release judgement of ourselves and others, release our commitment to perfection, we are able to enter into compassion. We soften. We open. We understand that life is bumpy, and we sit together, witnessing the unfolding of one moment to the next.

THE LITERAL MEANING OF THE WORD COMPASSION is 'to suffer or endure with'. However, passion doesn't just mean suffering, the root of the word, but celebration and joy as well. The American Episcopal priest and theologian Matthew Fox writes, 'Compassion operates at the same level as celebration because what is of most moment in compassion is not feelings of pity but feelings of togetherness.'[23]

When we are able to step out of the chatter and clinging of our ego-mind, we are able to be with someone more fully. This might look like crying with a friend who has lost a loved one, or playing blocks with a toddler, or sitting with a sensation in the pit of your stomach without judgement.

Compassion is the opposite of trying to fix someone. It is the opposite of judgement, pity, or shutting down in the face of discomfort. Compassion can feel vulnerable, and when we feel vulnerable our response is to protect ourselves. Sometimes this response is necessary for survival. But as we grow spiritually and emotionally, we can experience vulnerability without losing ourselves. When we do, miracles happen.

The Nature of Compassion

When a child falls and scrapes her knees, her adult might respond by scolding her for crying, insisting that she is fine. This response comes from a fear of being vulnerable. We don't want to feel another's pain. We have the experience of having been there, knowing that a scratched knee isn't really that big a deal. Yet when we give this response to a crying child, we shut down her response to life and her feelings.

When we respond with compassion, we don't, as we might fear, feed the drama. We simply sit with her by giving a hug, looking at the knee, looking in her eyes and acknowledging that it hurts. We might offer a gentle, unattached smile. She knows two things in this exchange — one, that she is okay (we are not panicking); and two, that her feelings and experiences matter to us.

Tears express that vulnerability in which we
can endure having our hearts broken and go right on
loving. In the tears flows a sweetness not of our own
making, which has been known in our tradition as the
Divine Mercy. Our jagged and hard-edged earth plane
is the realm in which this mercy is the most deeply,
excruciatingly, and beautifully released. That's our
business down here. That's what we're here for.

CYNTHIA BOURGEAULT [24]

This is the nature of compassion, to show another that they are not alone and that he or she matters. I often wonder what our world would look like were we humans able to respond with compassion to others and to events. Not just when it feels good to do so, as when we donate food to charities or send blankets to tsunami survivors, but when it is hard to do so. What would our world be were we able to sit with others, to endure with others, when our hard-edged plane brought us into excruciating pain? And then when we had others do the same for us? Were our world truly founded on compassion, our current economies, education systems, modes of power, and government would utterly collapse.

But for the moment, since such an idea is beyond the scope of this book, let us begin with ourselves, our families and our homes. How can we live more compassionately as parents?

Living Compassionately as Parents

First, we must learn to listen, to be open to what our children and partners have to say. Sometimes this brings up issues that are uncomfortable, so we need to be strong enough in ourselves to stay present and mindful of our reactions. By doing so, you tell your child (or partner) that he or she is important enough for you to endure discomfort to be present for them.

Second, we need to practise 'turning towards' our loved ones when they offer us a 'bid' for attention, affection, humour or support. When our child says excitedly, 'Look

what I built', we need to look up from the smart phone and look at what they built. Studies on healthy relationships found that people who turn towards their loved ones' 'bids' for attention yield greater emotional connection, passion and joy in their relationships.

Thirdly, we must seek to heal our own barriers to compassion. These barriers can come in so many forms: depression, busyness, the need for attention, beliefs about how attention 'spoils' a child, and so on. If you notice yourself turning away from your child or stifling his or her uncomfortable feelings like anger, take some time to meditate, write in a journal or speak with a therapist about what lies beneath these fears or habits. What does anger mean to you? What does attention signify to you? What do you fear by sitting with your child's jagged edges? With your own?

When we can learn to sit with our own and others' jagged edges, which we achieve through mindfulness, we can begin to transform our whole planet.

Compassion is a way of being at home in the universe, with life and with death, with the seen and the unseen. The energy-consciousness that compassion presumes takes one beyond mere psychologies and spiritualities of inter-personalism.

MATTHEW FOX [25]

CHAPTER FIVE

BECOMING WHOLE

The Hero returns home, having faced her demons. She continues to integrate the lessons she learned on her journey, for learning and growth are never-ending. Now, however, she may become a guide for others on their journeys of transformation. She has gained greater compassion for herself and for others. She is learning to nurture herself while supporting those around her. Her tools are creativity, playfulness, and the ever-enlightening teacher, awareness.

CREATIVITY

I sit with my growing children, letting my mind quiet. I breathe and become present to my beating heart. In moments like these, I am sometimes overwhelmed by the moment blooming into creation. To me, this is God or the Tao, the force of love that creates everything. I am called to participate by creating, too.

WE ARE CREATIVE BEINGS, every one of us. For some, creative energy is expressed through painting, writing, dancing. In others, the creative impulse is expressed through cooking or crafting a marketing plan or decorating a beautiful home. Many times I've heard people say they just aren't creative, but I actually don't think that's possible. By our very existence, we flow from the Tao. We are formed of Nature. We are all creative beings.

Children can teach us a lot about being creative. Watch small children play with building blocks or dolls or sticks and grass, and observe the human brain creating. Creating is in itself a form of meditation, for in order to create we must quiet the inner critic, at least for a time, and let creation flow through us. In the flow experience, we become fully alive. It no longer matters how tired we are, or what kind of a hair day we are having, or that we need to take out the rubbish and schedule a dentist appointment. We become present, the chatter quiets, and we create.

In this space we can come to know a little sliver of the vast power of creation present in the universe. We come to know the joy, the agony, the frustration, and the fire of creation. Through this process we come to know ourselves better, and to develop some understanding of others as well.

Mindful Creativity

You have no doubt heard the idea that how you do one thing is how you do everything. I think this is particularly true of creativity – and also, of parenting (a very creative act). If you consider yourself an artist, or you have some creative activity you like to do, notice how you do this thing. Notice:

- What are your habits and patterns as you work?
- What do you tell yourself while you dance, paint, cook, write, sew, etc?
- What do you discover and learn?
- How do these patterns reflect on the rest of your life?

If you don't think of yourself as a creative person, try this: colour with your children, or build with Lego, or craft fairy houses out of twigs and pine cones and acorns. As you do, practise mindfulness. There is no wrong or right way here, just noticing. Here are a few questions to ask without judgement as you colour or play with your children.

We come to know ourselves better, and to develop some understanding of others as well.

• WHAT DO YOU NOTICE YOURSELF FEELING, SAYING, AND WONDERING? Notice when you feel bored, restless, or judgemental of yourself or the creative process. After a while of noticing and letting go, does a curiosity step in? How does this shift your focus and how you feel about the activity? Notice if there are moments of joy, or moments where you feel what you are doing is 'good' art. None of these feelings is better or worse, but all give you information about yourself and your relationship to creativity.

• DO YOU WANT TO CONTROL YOUR CHILDREN'S DRAWING? Be aware of when you want to step in and control what your children are doing, when you feel you can make something better. Many people think they are not creative because they cannot create a sonata or a museum-worthy masterpiece as soon as they sit down. Creativity isn't about perfection or product, although the creative process can yield these things over time. Creativity is about openness and curiosity. It is about being open to what happens and letting it take its own time. Controlling your creative process or someone else's is about fear of the power we all possess to create.

• DO YOU LET YOURSELF BE FREE AND CURIOUS? Our culture focuses so much on external, tangible things. Verifiable proof. So much of curiosity (and also parenting!) is invisible, internal, and even mysterious. Many authors, for instance, talk about how their characters tell them what to write. As soon as a person thinks this approach to creating is crazy or silly, it shuts down. When we are free and curious, something happens. Creativity awakens. We scare it away when we start analysing (creating is different from editing, a wholly different process – here I am talking about flow and creating).

• WHAT DO YOU DISCOVER ABOUT YOURSELF? When I first start a project, I feel full of energy and promise. Then, a few weeks into writing a book, or a few hours into sewing a costume, or a few days into a new job, I get really depressed. It's not a conscious thing; I noticed this pattern after writing several books. If I let the process just sit there, I notice that my depression comes from overwhelm and the mess of digging deeper into a project. The depression usually lifts on its own as my semi-conscious and conscious minds make sense of the project. Since I have noticed this and explored the underlying fears, it has mostly lifted. What happens when you create?

• HOW CAN THESE DISCOVERIES HELP YOU BE A MORE PATIENT, COMPASSIONATE PARENT? Parenting is a very creative process. How you do other creative endeavours will show you something about how you parent. I have learned over time, for instance, how my books come about. They begin with obsessive planning and outlining. Then research. Then I start filling in the outline with what I have discovered. Eventually I hit a flow space where I let the project have a life of its own, but my planning and organizing mind steps in now and then with course corrections. To my amusement, this is pretty much how I parent, too. But as a parent I often have to let go of all that research and planning, and just live in relationship instead of trying to create my children or their lives. When I step back from trying to plan and organize them, I become much more patient and open.

• DO YOU LONG TO BE MORE CREATIVE? If you are a closet artist, look for ways that allow your creativity out into the sunlight. Trust yourself! A good way to begin is to just play more with your children – not forcing yourself to play that game you can't stand, but doing something together that you both enjoy. Collaging, colouring with crayons or scented markers, gardening, cooking, and journaling or scrapbooking are ways to let your inner artist play without (too much) fear. A classic book dedicated to this process is Julia Cameron's *The Artist's Way*. A parenting book that can bring more creativity and play into your parenting relationship is *Playful Parenting* by Lawrence J. Cohen.

Creativity is our birthright. I invite you to unlearn any restrictions you carry about creating. Notice how these restrictions – or lack thereof – help you parent. Notice how, when you let them go in you and in your expectations in your children, you all become much lighter and more joyful.

PLAYTIME EXERCISE

MANDALAS

The mandala is a tool for meditation using the circle as a focus. Mandalas consist of concentric circles and other shapes radiating outward from the centre. Creating a mandala can also be a fun creative activity to do with your children. Mandala colouring books or pages printed from the Internet are the easiest way to play with mandalas in any setting.

You might want to breathe mindfully for a few moments before colouring, or just pull the colouring sheets out when you need something to do, like at the doctor's office or on a rainy day. You can draw your own back-and-forth mandalas by taking turns. You start with a circle shape, then your child draws flowers around this centre, then you draw a squiggly snake around the flowers, and so on, back and forth, adding concentric circles as you go.

Mandalas can also be created on a nature walk or in the garden using seasonally available items — digging in the sand at the beach, poking icicles into the snow, or making spirals of leaves and pine cones on the ground. The practice is intended to be both meditation and creation.

NURTURING

◆

As parents, especially if we are the full-time caregiver, we tend to forget to nurture ourselves. We are so busy that self-care gets shunted to the lowest spot on the list of priorities. When this goes on too long, however, we suffer, and everyone else suffers with us. When Mama (or Papa) ain't happy, ain't nobody happy.

NURTURING OURSELVES actually nurtures others, as well. You've no doubt heard the aeroplane analogy: give yourself the oxygen mask first, flight attendants tell us every time we fly, and then attend to your children. If we do it the other way around, as is our instinct, we will black out and die. We know this. But day to day, when we're not in a life-or-death situation, we so often come last. How can we meet all our commitments yet still care for ourselves?

Sometimes we don't even notice how utterly drained we are. One night, many years ago, I allowed myself to leave my new baby daughter for the first time. I left her at home with her dad, tucked extra nursing pads in my bag, and headed across town to meet some friends. Four other mothers and I met for a spa party at MoonDance Botanicals, an independently owned herb shop. A little bell jingled as I pushed open the heavy wooden door. The cosy shop smelled divine – herb sachets and hand-made soaps lay nestled in artsy clay bowls and atop antique wooden pedestals. Felt and glitter fairies danced on a little tree at the front counter. Tiny white pixie lights twinkled along the walls. Just entering the shop, I felt my shoulders let go of some of the tension I hadn't even realized I was carrying.

MoonDance spa parties consist of rubbing a series of handmade and totally decadent salves, scrubs and creams into your skin. After cleansing our faces with apricot cream, we leaned over individual bowls of boiling water scented with a handful of carefully chosen herbs, a towel draped over our heads to trap in the healing, spicy steam. At this point, the last layer of new-mother tension melted from my shoulders. Tears pricked my eyes. It was like when someone performs for you some random act of kindness and you cry from joy and a realization that you really needed that touching act of love. I later wrote, 'It was as if through the message of these sweet-scented herbs and the fire of the purified steam, a goddess had laid a hand on my shoulder and ensured me all would be all right. I would survive the spiritual initiation of motherhood, from the sleepless nights to round-the-clock nursing and the search for my own private self in the midst of a new identity.'[26]

We can literally forget ourselves and not realize we've done so.

Day to day... we so often come last.
How can we meet all our commitments
yet still care for ourselves?

PLAYTIME EXERCISE

HERBAL FACE STEAM

✳

This is for yourself, but if you have children old enough to sit still you may want to involve them. Find a time when you will not be disturbed for at least twenty minutes. That is possible! You will need a large bowl, boiling water from a kettle, and your favourite herbs. Good ones for soothing include lavender, rose petals, calendula, comfrey, chamomile and rosemary. For nurturing the immune system, include some thyme or oregano. Orange peel is rejuvenating. Cedarwood calms anxiety. You will need a handful or two of dried herbs, or just a few drops of essential oils (go easy – they can overwhelm!). Also gather a clean bath towel. Put the herbs in the bowl on a table, and pour the hot water over the herbs. Sit in front of the bowl and cover your head and the bowl with the towel to trap in the healing steam. Sit further away from the bowl if it's too hot; as the water cools, you may want to add more hot water. Sit with your head over the bowl for at least fifteen minutes, breathing in the steam and meditating by being present and following your breath. When finished, pour the herbs on the garden (unless you put oils in it; don't put the herbs down a drain as they can clog it), and rub a soothing lotion into your skin.

Ways to Care for Yourself

What do you do to take care of yourself? Here are some other ideas for self-care; choose something that makes sense for you or see if these ideas generate some of your own:

- Take a brisk walk by yourself.
- Take a bubble bath or a bath with Epsom salts in it.
- Get a massage, even a short chair massage.
- Trade child care with a friend and do something you enjoy, like seeing a film, going to an art gallery, or just getting a cup of coffe and reading.
- Do yoga or take a class in something that interests you.
- Go to the gym or work out in another way that you enjoy.
- Get up fifteen minutes or half an hour before your family for some quiet time.
- Have a girls' (or boys') night out – meet friends for a glass of wine, or go to a gallery opening together, or find a herbal shop that has a spa party!
- Let yourself sleep in at least one day a week.
- Hire a cleaning service a few times a year and use the time to do whatever you like.

Listen to Your Body

A year and a half ago, all I wanted to do was stay in bed and read a book all day. Of course I didn't let myself do this, as I had a three-year-old and a seven-year-old to care for (by the way, it doesn't matter if you work or stay home with your children, if they are at school or taught at home, all mothers – all parents – feel spread too thin and overwhelmed). A few weeks later, my adrenals made me lie in bed and do nothing all day. I was having panic attacks and hypoglycaemic episodes. The result of not slowing down, mixed with the hormonal storm of weaning my son, was severe adrenal fatigue. I wasn't putting my own oxygen mask on first.

Listen to your body. When it says Stop!, you need to stop. I know it feels impossible. We mums (especially, but dads, too) have wrapped up our sense of worth in how well we perform as mothers. Slowing down to care for myself is anathema to proving my worth to the world at large. But if we don't slow down, we will crash, and then who will care for the children? My husband had to take a week off work when my crash finally hit because I literally couldn't parent. Or do much of anything else.

When I do care for myself, which includes small things like face steams and bigger things like getting my sister-in-law or mother to take the children for an afternoon, I sometimes have to struggle with a bit of guilt. But then I am a better

---

◆

When we take time-out for ourselves, even for
only a few minutes, the struggling parts inside us know
that someone cares, someone is paying attention.
CHERI HUBER AND MELINDA GUYOL, 'TIME OUT FOR PARENTS'[27]

◆

---

mother and a better person. And I don't have to spend all day in bed. It may be something of a cliché, but it's so very true: in order to nurture others, we must be nurtured. Take a deep breath, and write a list now of ways you can care for yourself and ask for nurturing from your support people. And if you don't have support people? It's time to get some, my friend. You cannot do this alone. That's not a failure, it's a fact.

COOPERATION

Life is ultimately about working together. Cooperation and connection underlie all healthy systems: natural habitats, gut flora, nursery classrooms, and families. By teaching our children about the strength found in cooperation, we help make the world healthier and stronger as well. We all benefit from connection and cooperation.

FINNISH SCHOOLS RECENTLY ROCKED the international education world by excelling in both national test scores and employment rates. Countries like Japan and the US, hungry for such accolades, looked to Finland to discover their secret. Then they scratched their heads in wonder, for the secret to successful education in Finland was twofold: equality and cooperation, ideas that don't really 'fit' in Japanese or US culture (we like to think they do, but in reality we're very competitive and hierarchical). In Finnish schools, all children are given the best education possible, all free. Policymakers, teachers and administrators work together to meet each child's needs. Teachers are given freedom to craft their own lessons. They are given the power to run their classrooms. And students in those classrooms are required to support each other in cooperative learning.

I value this model as a way to run a family. Whenever my children whine about doing chores, they get my standard line: 'Everyone in our family helps out. It's part of being in our family.' We work together, we all get things we like and have to do things we don't like. When we support each other and all pitch in for daily needs such as cleaning, cooking, or caring for pets, we each have the freedom and opportunity to follow the pursuits that make us who we are. My daughter can focus on her drawing, computer animation and gaming, and gymnastics. My son these days loves Lego. He loves to build and create. My pursuits include reading a lot, writing, gardening, and planning teaching activities. My husband enjoys watching American football (the Packers), playing music and writing poetry. These are the activities that make us who we are, but we can only do them when we all cooperate to get the needs of daily living covered first.

Cooperation is what

makes equality possible.

JUKKA SARJALA[28]

Good Communication

In our family, we parents are in charge, but we are not more important than our children. Our children, in turn, are respected as individuals free to grow into themselves, but they do not get to run the show, either. What makes this work for us, besides an understanding my husband and I share that our children are their own persons whose votes count for something, is communication. Communication needs to come from 'right speech', or the idea that words must come from the understanding that all beings are connected and we must strive to do no harm.

Good communication in a family requires:

- That it is safe to speak your truth.
- That each person's perspective is respected.
- That when we talk we follow certain guidelines like using 'I' statements (a way to honour yourself, take responsibility for your feelings and reactions, and do no harm).
- And that you know what you even need to say!

In many families, it is not safe to speak up without getting blamed or shamed. If you grew up in a family like this, or you find it sneaking into your current family, meditation and therapy can help you look at the uncomfortable underlying fears and habits that perpetuate this unsafe environment. This is beyond the scope of this book, but it underlies everything I have written about. Mindful parenting requires the healing of old patterns of shame.

Compassionate Communication

A good resource for respectful communication is Non-Violent Communication, http://www.cnvc.org. The website contains videos, articles, trainings and books. Non-Violent Communication is a valuable tool for any parent, teacher or person who works in groups.

I Hear You

Each person's perspective being respected doesn't mean everyone is 'right', but that everyone has the right to speak up. Learning to acknowledge or validate others' feelings, especially when you don't agree with them, is an extremely valuable tool. This can be as simple as listening and repeating back what you understand the person is saying. Practise in the little moments so that when tension is high, it is an easier habit to validate others. For instance, when my son wants another Lego Mixels set and I am not going to buy one that day, I simply say, 'I hear that you want a Mixels.' Or 'I hear that you want more sugar right now.' Then when you are arguing with your teenager or your partner, it is more natural to say, 'I hear what you are saying – you are angry that I came home late without calling.' Or whatever.

> *Learn to acknowledge or validate others' feelings.*

The 'I' Statement

Another simple but effective tool to get in the habit of using is 'I' statements. This means you take responsibility for your feelings and speak from your perspective. It can feel stilted and fake at first but is a very powerful shift in communication and cooperative living. The basic formula for an 'I' statement is 'I feel ... when you ... because ...'. So, say you've asked your son to take out the rubbish, again, and he is whining about doing so, again. You say, 'I feel frustrated when you argue with me about the rubbish and forget to take it out because it feels disrespectful and ignores our family agreements.' You own your feelings, you state clearly what the situation is without blaming, and then you identify (for him and yourself!) what the problem really is.

Communicate with Mindfulness

Sometimes the challenge in cooperative, respectful communication is that you don't know what you feel, what you want, and why you feel what you feel. Here's where mindfulness (and sometimes therapy, journaling, or talking with a trusted friend) can help. Some people know exactly what they are feeling and what words to put to those sensations and emotions. Many people do not. Taking time to check in will bring you clarity and help you communicate more clearly and respectfully with others. This is especially true when you find yourself reacting to a situation and don't know why.

Use mindfulness, meditation and awareness to tune in to what you are feeling. Use this knowledge to create more open, respectful communication and an environment of cooperation and respect. Your whole family will be healthier, happier, and better able to handle life's many challenges, not unlike Finland's confident and well-educated students who are raised on equality and cooperation.

CURIOSITY

◆

Children are curious about what will happen if they pour water onto soil or poke the cat or put a stick in front of a crawling bug. We sometimes try to turn our children's exploring into a learning moment by asking probing questions. But open, simple curiosity has a value all its own.

CURIOUS MINDFULNESS OCCURS when you sit in meditation, observing your breath. This curiosity has no agenda except to be aware. A sensation arises, and we look at it. *What are you?* we ask, watching and feeling. In meditation we don't have the same intensity that a curious child has, we have more of a soft focus. But we are equally open to whatever arises.

Curious mindfulness is a powerful practice not only on the meditation cushion, but when you are in a situation that causes anxiety or distress. Instead of trying to stop an uncomfortable feeling, we can just be curious about it. Without being attached to any outcome, I can be curious about the clenching in the pit of my stomach when I am overcome with irrational anxiety. I can be curious about a habit, like chewing on my cheek or biting my nail. I can witness my anger or irritation with my children.

Unpleasantness Isn't Going to Kill Us

Curiosity about an unpleasant sensation gives us a bit of distance without disassociating. I am still all there, having my feelings and sensations. Yet simultaneously there is another part of me, my Witness, that is watching what happens. When I cultivate this kind of curiosity, I invariably discover something about myself or the situation that I probably would not have seen while wrapped up in my reactions and egoistic mind. I notice my resistance to what is happening, or my fears about possible outcomes. I sit with those observations, not condemning or trying to change, just noticing. Often this non-judgemental curiosity leads to a release of the tension I am feeling, but not always. That release isn't the point, but sometimes it is an outcome.

Curiosity about an unpleasant feeling shows us that the unpleasantness isn't going to kill us. Obviously I'm not talking about when you are actually in danger; we do what needs to be done to get away from the growling dog or the speeding bus. When the feeling of anxiety or anger isn't tied to a real threat, however, we need to notice how it is just a sensation. Then we can begin to take responsibility for our feelings. We can begin to notice all the layers behind a sensation or a feeling. Like Jane Goodall patiently waiting to see what the chimpanzees did, we sit and discover layer after layer about ourselves without trying to control, direct or manage.

What we discover is that we are not our feelings. Emotions are our energetic responses to a situation. They are real and valid. They are not who we *are*, though. Who I am is much more nebulous than even an emotion. We can begin to find what that is, that true self, by first noticing what we think we are – identity, feelings, relationships – and then noticing that we are not those things, but something greater.

This discovery of curiosity about feelings and sensations can be liberating for an adult, but also for children, who can be utterly consumed with emotions.

Cultivate an Open Curiosity

What happens when you are curious about your feelings, sensations, or an experience? Next time you find yourself resisting something or rushing through an experience, try to cultivate curiosity. Sitting at the doctor's office, playing Lego or superheroes or dolls with your children, driving in stop-and-go traffic: these are all opportunities to cultivate curiosity and awareness of what is actually happening right now in this moment. What happens next?

PLAYTIME EXERCISE

FREEZE & FEEL

You might want to try this on your own first, or do it with your children. Have your children move around in an open space like the sitting room or garden. They can dance, sway scarves, or walk around. When you clap or ring a small bell, they are to freeze and tune in to what they are feeling. They might notice tight muscles, tingling in their arms, a breeze on their skin, a lingering taste in their mouth from lunch, or even a light sense of joy. Talk about how *emotions* are felt through *sensation*. What sensations are they experiencing right now? Be curious about all of your sensations. Begin moving again, then ring the bell or clap, and notice. Freeze, and feel. Do this a few times, taking turns ringing the bell, then discuss what you have all discovered.

Another place to cultivate an open curiosity is with our children when they are doing something we don't like. Allow yourself to be curious about your child's feelings and reactions. What is it they need, or think they need? How is this translating into behaviours? Again, we act first to protect a child's safety when necessary, but once he is safe, we can sit in open curiosity. I find that when I am open to my child's behaviour, instead of controlling, stopping or judging the behaviour, I develop at the very least more patience. Often a sense of compassion grows in me, rather than anger and irritation. Curiosity usually leads us to discovery, as well.

Being curious about my child's behaviour doesn't usually look, however, like asking her *why* she is doing or feeling something. Asking a child 'Why did you do that?' implies that she has done something wrong. The answer is invariably 'I don't know' mixed with shame. Instead, I have to wait for clarity and discovery. When I am open, using all my senses to patiently and non-judgementally observe my child's behaviour, usually after a while some sort of glimmer of understanding arises spontaneously. Then I might check in (depending on the age of the child): 'I'm thinking that maybe you are feeling really angry right now because you don't want me to go out tonight.' Or whatever. This opens the gentle door for a child to say what she needs and what she is afraid of. We can only get to that safe place, though, when we cultivate openness through curiosity.

RESPONSIBILITY

◆

Taking responsibility for all our actions and emotions is a form of centredness. It requires both strength and vulnerability. It requires divesting ourselves of any fears about standing tall in the face of truth, no matter how uncomfortable. Taking responsibility is a mindfulness practice that we can model and teach to our children.

HAVE YOU EVER NOTICED that blaming actually makes a person avoid responsibility? When we look to find fault, we create a game of mental hot potato, where each person is eager to toss the blame and shame on to someone else. This is true of adults but is especially evident in children, who have to fight for a sense of power in an adult world. We say, 'Who left the ice cream out on the worktop?' or 'Did you hit your sister?' The immediate and visceral response to such questions, which are usually tinged with anger or threat, is to shrink. To hide. And to look desperately and quickly to where you might either shed the blame or come up with a good excuse. An excuse is simply a way to excuse yourself from the shame and blame.

What we parents and other adults of power in a child's life really want to do is to teach our children responsibility. The ability to respond to a situation and make right what is wrong is a very mature skill. It also takes a huge amount of self-possession and strength. Picture a politician or administrator standing up and accepting responsibility for a mistake. They are strong and grounded, and they make eye contact. Many people can't actually stand tall in the face of such a challenge. Again picture the policymaker or police officer avoiding blame, feeling shame, shifting his or her eyes and shuffling uncomfortably. Such a scene reminds me of a child being chastised. By shooting children down with blame, we do not build in them this strength of responsibility; in fact, we teach them to hide and shirk responsibility whenever possible.

Supported, Loved & Safe

What does a person need to take responsibility? First, she needs to know that even if she did something wrong, she is still loved. Her needs will still be met — she will be supported, loved, and safe. Second, to take responsibility rather than just feel at fault, a person needs to be able to identify, by herself or with help, what needs to happen to make something right. Finally, she needs to be supported while she makes things right.

A person needs to be able to identify, by himself or with help, what needs to happen to make something right.

Creating this situation takes practice. We parents are so attached to our agendas that when something gets in the way — a spilled cup of tea, knocked heads from play-fighting, a broken vase – we immediately get angry. The child in us feels personally blocked by the problem, and we quickly jump to assess both why the situation is a problem and what our child did to cause the problem. We immediately jump to 'Ack! If only you hadn't done that, my life would go smoothly!' What a burden for a poor child to carry! The question to ask ourselves (rather than jump to shame about what crummy parents we are – that is not the point!) is: 'What does it mean to me that my life needs to run smoothly?'

Losing Control

Take a minute and feel into this. You are hurrying to get out the door. Get the children to school, yourself to work, drop off the dry cleaning on the way, can't find your keys. Your youngest is sitting on the floor with her shoes next to her, smearing porridge on the floor.

Did your blood pressure rise just a little as you read that? In the adult world, this is a very real problem. We have deadlines and schedules. We are expected to be clean, on time, and fairly well put together. Children don't usually care about these things. However, while we acknowledge that this is a problem, we might also peek into why it causes us so much distress, which we then put on to our children.

For me, underneath the stress and reaction is a fear that I am going to screw up. I will look bad and be judged by other adults as being not quite together enough. As being not enough. I will be laughed at or shamed. There is also a layer of self-importance: my schedule, my plan, all these things I have created or bought into in order to feel in control of things becomes more important than a loving relationship with my child.

For me, and perhaps also for you, this is key: I do so much each day in order to feel in control.

Admitting that I do not ultimately have control over the unfolding of life is terrifying. Much of what we are trying to control, usually, is a sense of vulnerability. We are so afraid of being hurt, shamed, or abandoned. We want at all costs to avoid feeling vulnerable.

Setting an Example

What needs to happen in a situation like this, a response that requires mindfulness, is to notice my reaction. Breathe. Take responsibility for my feelings of impatience, vulnerability, stress and lack of control. Hand the child a cloth to wipe up the porridge (or call in the dog!) and ask her – again – calmly to put on her shoes because it's time to go. I have to take responsibility for my frustration that she should have done it the first time or should know not to paint with porridge (at least not on the floor). Only when we begin to take responsibility for our own feelings and reactions can we stop putting them on others. Then we set an example for our children, who can see what it looks like to take responsibility for actions or feelings. In turn, they can take responsibility themselves without fear of our dumping our reactions and blame on to them. They feel safe and we can all stand in our own power. Not power over others or the universe, but the only power we ultimately ever possess, which is the power of owning who we are and what we do in the world. From this place of centred power, a place that requires strength and mindfulness, we can have a clear ability to respond to the world around us, which ultimately is what responsibility is all about.

AWARENESS

Awareness and attention: actions that bring us back to the present moment. These are practices that we must continue returning to again and again. They are at the heart of all that we have explored in these pages. They are simple, yet deeply transformative. Enter awareness. Be here now.

THE CHILDREN CALL AND SPLASH in the fountains, and I wave and smile from the shade of a young tree. We had learned that morning that our beloved orange kitten had been hit by a car. We had all cried, and lit a candle on the family altar, next to which we placed a drawing of little Puck. Despite the heat and my fatigue, I knew we needed to get out, but I didn't have energy for anything big, and we didn't have any extra money to spend. So I suggested the library, and

◆

We can handle anything when we exchange

our worries and fears for alertness and spontaneity,

when we focus solely on what is in front of us.

KAREN MAEZEN MILLER [29]

◆

---

before that, some time at the two fountains in the middle of the shopping area next door.

Toddlers with saggy nappies and wide-brimmed hats collected water in take-away cups, pouring it contentedly on to the hot pavement. Music played from speakers nestled beneath the trees. Serious-looking little girls in pink bathing suits climbed the stone steps of one of the fountains. Mothers chatted over iced coffee and nannies peered at their charges through stylish sunglasses.

My daughter kneeled in the deeper of the two fountains and dipped her fringe in the water, transfixed by her dripping hair. My son pulled up the legs of his shorts, trying not to get too wet. I sat and watched the children from the shade with my mix of thoughts and feelings as they slid past like clouds in a windy sky. Sadness at the loss of our cat, paired with a streak of guilt from a secret relief that I had one less being to care for. Curiosity about the little girl who looked like she might have Down's syndrome. Joy at her open smile as she splashed about in the water. Boredom as my own children played. An almost overwhelming gratitude and love as my daughter looked up from her strange hair play in the water and waved at me. Thoughts about their upcoming birthday party, and where we might have it. Worries about money. Peace as I had the luxury to sit and breathe and enjoy the warm afternoon in a safe, lovely area. A question as to what I would make for dinner that night.

My thoughts turned to this book. I allowed my thoughts and feelings to drift away, noticing them and then releasing them as I slipped into mindfulness. As I became present to the moment, I settled into the sweet joy of the Now.

Awareness of the Moment

I recently read an article whining about how 'mindfulness' has become the latest fad, and how this fad is fooling people into believing that if only they breathe and relax, all the world's problems will go away. The author felt that the rising popularity of meditation was just the latest money-making fad, touted as a cure-all for medical ailments and restless children. She used the words 'the cult of mindfulness'.

I felt for the poor author. I'm no stranger to the snarky feeling in response to the latest fad. But mindfulness and meditation only falls into this category of faddish cult when it is misunderstood. And it so often is, sadly, because it's held on a pedestal of cool. When something is sentimentalized and romanticized, it does become a fad doomed to failure. But as any 'happily' married person knows, when you really look at the nitty gritty of your spouse, the pimples and nose hair and anger and irritation – the romanticism goes away, but is replaced by an experience that goes deeper than words and is worth so much more than the sentimental roses of before. The same is true of mindfulness. The author of this article clearly hasn't experienced real awareness of the moment. She doesn't see how it isn't about relaxation or peace. Mindfulness can lead to relaxation and a sense of abiding peace – but these aren't the point of practice.

The point of awareness is awareness. Just like the point of parenting is to raise children. To love, experience, create.

All of our other expectations and fears and spinning around in circles, that's just life. But we have a choice to inhabit what is, this moment, this love, pure and simple.

CELEBRATION

Celebration is about feelings of togetherness as we pause to honour what is, what has been, and what is yet to come. Celebrating life from a connected and joy-filled place lays the foundations for compassionate living. Celebration is an invitation to become present while cultivating joy and gratitude.

WHEN MY DAUGHTER WAS TWO YEARS OLD, we made a yule log out of a small log, red ribbon, collected pine cones, and the ever-handy glue gun. We gathered around the fire pit in our back yard on the night of 21 December, burning this home-made yule log. There was old, crunchy snow on the ground and the air was below 20 degrees Fahrenheit, but we felt cosy with our little fire. As the almost full moon rose in the east, I felt solidarity with my ancestors, who kept warm around an actual fire all winter long; they didn't have the luxury of central heating or electricity. I felt grateful for my home, for electricity and gas, and for fire as ritual and fun, not necessity. I felt the calm joy of celebrating simple things with my daughter, the moon, and a fire.

The next day we awoke at dawn – not for ritual or to honour the birth of the Sun, but because when she was a toddler, my daughter woke with the sun every morning. But it being the Solstice, I allowed myself to enjoy this early rising. I watched the pink sky, and felt joy and gratitude at the Rebirth of the Sun, of the day, of myself reborn each day.

Celebrating the Small Moments

I find that celebrating the little things, as well as the seasons as they are, helps ground me in the present. Part of my path as a parent includes celebrating the Wheel of the Year: the solstices, equinoxes, and the four holidays at cross quarters with these solar events. We celebrate snowfall, the first spring flower, the harvest moon. We celebrate the usual holidays, too. And we celebrate little things, like chickadees at the bird feeder, a beautiful full moon, a goal set and met.

The celebrations of small moments don't have to be grand. I might read a poem and prepare a special snack — apples in autumn, hot chocolate after we play in the snow, or a peach perfectly ripe from the farmers' market. Little activities like this help to ground us, and they also honour and affirm the life all around us. By slowing down, celebrating, and witnessing the unfolding of each moment, we honour our fellow animals, the wind, the sky and the land. This gives us a sense of place in the grander scheme of life. It reminds us to look for the positive and take joy in small blessings.

Let your celebrations, whether for a birthday or the first harvested spring radish, be centred around mindfulness. Focus on senses: the scent of a lit candle, a song at bedtime, the sweetness of a strawberry, a blue feather found in the snow. Let these sensations be a call to being present. I find that when I am fully present, a sensation of celebration of the moment naturally arises. This is not a big to-do, but rather a quiet joy felt at my centre. My goal is to make all our celebrations centred on this simple pleasure of life shared.

Every moment is a death

Of all that has gone before,

And a birth

Of all that is to come.

WILLIAM MARTIN [30]

NAMASTE

I hope my thoughts and meditations have inspired greater awareness of your path as a parent, and therefore your own Hero's Journey. We learn so much about ourselves and each other simply by being present to what is. In the process, a wisdom arises like sunlight in the east. This wisdom, this mindfulness, will affect every area of your life. It will make you a better parent, though that's not really the point. It will help you raise more balanced and healthy kids. It may even lead to greater personal health, and even to improved planetary health. For as we become more aware and present, fear, anger and violence lose their power over us. We become clearer as to our most basic nature, which is good and right and infinite. And breath by breath we are able to live from this clear space a little bit more each day.

ENDNOTES

1. 'Parenting with Mindful Awareness', Myla and Jon Kabat-Zinn, in *Finding Your Inner Mama*, ed. Eden Steinberg, p92 (Trumpeter, Boston & London, 2007)

2. Ibid.

3. Louis C.K. on *Conan*, 2009. Accessed video at https://www.youtube.com/uEY58fiSK8E December 2014.

4. *Zen Mind, Beginner's Mind,* Shunryu Suzuki, p38 (Weatherhill, New York, 1980)

5. *Everyday Zen,* Charlotte Joko Beck, p11 (HarperSanFrancisco, New York, 1989)

6. *The Gifts of Imperfection: Let Go of Who You Think You're Supposed to Be and Embrace Who You Are,* Brené Brown, p53 (Hazelden, Center City, MN, 2010)

7. *Everyday Zen,* Charlotte Joko Beck, p82 (HarperSanFrancisco, New York, 1989)

8. *Women's Bodies, Women's Wisdom,* Christiane Northrup, p604 (Bantam Books, New York, 1998)

9. Quoted in *Everyday Zen,* Charlotte Joko Beck, p82 (HarperSanFrancisco, New York, 1989)

10. *Hand Wash Cold: Care Instructions for an Ordinary Life,* Karen Maezen Miller, p77 (New World Library, San Francisco, 2010)

11. *Women's Bodies, Women's Wisdom,* Christiane Northrup, p632 (Bantam Books, New York, 1998)

12. *Everyday Zen,* Charlotte Joko Beck, p13 (HarperSanFrancisco, New York, 1989)

13. Nancy McDermott, quoted in *Free Range Kids: How to Raise Safe, Self-Reliant Children (Without Going Nuts with Worry),* Lenore Skenerzy, p111 (Jossey-Bass, San Francisco, 2010)

14. *Zen Mind, Beginner's Mind,* Shunryu Suzuki, p38 (Weatherhill, New York, 1980)

15. *Women's Bodies, Women's Wisdom,* Christiane Northrup, p21 (Bantam Books, New York, 1998)

16. *Women's Bodies, Women's Wisdom,* Christiane Northrup, p64 (Bantam Books, New York, 1998)

17. 'Abandon Any Hope of Fruition', *Start Where You Are: A Guide to Compassionate Living,* Pema Chödrön, p96 (Shambhala, Boston & London, 1994)

18. 'I'm Breathing, Are You?', Nancy Hathaway, in *Finding Your Inner Mama,* ed. Eden Steinberg, p244 (Trumpeter, Boston & London, 2007)

19. *The Parent's Tao Te Ching: Ancient Advice for Modern Parents,* William Martin, p50 (Marlowe & Company, New York, 1999)

20. 'Meditation and the startle response: A case study', Robert W. Levenson; Paul Ekman; Matthieu Ricard; *Emotion*, Vol 12(3), Jun 2012, 650–658. Abstract accessed online December 2014 at http://psycnet.apa.org/journals/emo/12/3/650/

21. 'Effects of mindful-attention and compassion meditation training on amygdala response to emotional stimuli in an ordinary, non-meditative state', Gaëlle Desbordes; Lobsang T. Negi; Thaddeus W. W. Pace; et al, Frontiers in Human Neuroscience. 2012; 6: 292. Accessed online December 2014 at http://www.ncbi.nlm.nih.gov/pmc/articles/PMC3485650/ Published online Nov 1, 2012.

22. *Sex, Ecology, Spirituality: The Spirit of Evolution*, Ken Wilber, p257 (Shambhala, Boston & London, 1995)

23. *A Spirituality Named Compassion*, Matthew Fox, p4 (Harper & Row, San Francisco, 1979)

24. *The Wisdom Jesus*, Cynthia Bourgeault, p100 (Shambhala, Boston, 2008)

25. *A Spirituality Named Compassion*, Matthew Fox, p20 (Harper & Row, San Francisco, 1979)

26. 'Bolstering Breastfeeding', Clea Danaan in *Llewellyn's 2009 Herbal Almanac*, p114 (Llewellyn, Woodbury, MN, 2008)

27. 'Time Out for Parents', Cheri Huber and Melinda Guyol, in *Finding Your Inner Mama*, ed. Eden Steinberg, p240–241 (Trumpeter, Boston & London, 2007)

28. 'Equality and Cooperation: Finland's Path to Excellence', Jukka Sarjala, *American Educator*, Spring 2013, p32

29. *Momma Zen: Walking the Crooked Path of Motherhood*, Karen Maezen Miller, p25 (Trumpeter, Boston, 2006)

30. *The Parent's Tao Te Ching: Ancient Advice for Modern Parents*, William Martin, p127 (Marlowe & Company, New York, 1999)

INDEX

INDEX

ACKNOWLEDGEMENTS

Thank you to my readers,
Pilar and Dawn, for your help, support,
and insights. Thank you to my circle of Mamas
that keep me going. Thank you Sophie and Harper
for letting me write all sorts of things about you.
And of course, to Tony, for dancing the
journey with me.